Getting to Know YOU

Embrace your Unique Blueprint to
Make Decisions you Love and Trust
A Human Design Guidebook

By
Karen Flaherty

*Amy –
Be the you
you were meant
to be!

Karen*

Includes free Audio Book

Getting to Know YOU

Embrace your Unique Blueprint to Make Decisions you Love and Trust

A Human Design Guidebook

KAREN FLAHERTY

Disclaimer: Although in this book I present an overall view of Human Design, "Getting to Know YOU" is written from my personal perspective and is intended for educational purposes only. Nothing within the book should be taken as medical or mental health advice or seen as a substitute for the professional advice of a qualified medical practitioner. I encourage you throughout the book to work with your doctor and health-care providers, as needed. If in doubt, always consult a qualified health professional. Thank you!

Special thanks to Chaitanyo Taschler of The Human Design System and Erik Memmert of New Sunware Ltd. for their permission to use the quotes from Ra Uru Hu's audio tapes from 1999, which Chaitanyo taped, and the personally licensed Human Design charts within the book via New Sunware's software programs.

ISBN-13: 978-1-7325940-4-3

Advance praise for "Getting to Know YOU"

Whether you have just started your personal journey to make your life better (because it's not measuring up) or you have spent a fortune trying to find yourself and your life still isn't working the way you want, "Getting to Know YOU" is a must read. Karen has a fun, practical and engaging way of introducing you to your unique blueprint that will help you *play* life on your terms as you learn to make decisions you can trust and subsequently get what you want.

Annita Keane
Best Selling Author of "How Do I Know? Your Guide to Decision Making Mastery"
Founder of the "A" Game Academy, leading women to brilliance without burnout

When I read this book, I already had an understanding of Human Design for the past five years or so. This book had a lightness to it that I hadn't originally felt when I first heard about Human Design. The terms and jargon can feel heavy, but this had a light feel that allowed me to get back into it and smooth out some of the concepts I was confused about.

Rita Bielka
Founder, Happy Catalyst

Conversationally written, the author offers that all-important support to the reader—she gives you the confidence to try new things! She's telling you *her* story and leading you to recognize yours in an intimate, trusting, thought-provoking setting. She explores questions common to all of us—and provides the answers! This is a "how-to" book and then some!

Susan Slater, author
Ben Pecos and Dan Mahoney mystery series

"Getting to Know YOU" is one of the most refreshing books written on Human Design! Karen takes a complex, dense topic and brings it to life, explaining in practical and clear terms how knowing your unique Human Design can forever improve your life. Thank you, Karen!

Linda Albright
Founder, Women's Wealth Revolution

This book is user-friendly, practical, and a real page-turner that will assist anyone on a mission to understand their uniqueness and work with it, instead of fighting against or trying to suppress it. "Getting to Know YOU" addresses what we all want - to know, accept, and master our own psyche, mindset, and emotions so we can fully enjoy our lives, achieve success as each of defines it, and experience more ease, peace, and grace in the process. Karen provides a masterful guide for this insight into ourselves.

Sue Urda, Feel Good Guidess and Co-Founder of Powerful You!

I have had the most wonderful opportunity to be able to read Karen Flaherty's newest work, *"Getting to Know YOU: Embrace your Unique Blueprint to Make Decisions you Love and Trust – A Human Design Guidebook",* and it amazing. It is interesting to listen to people who want so badly to know what the future is, and how to get there. This book is their answer. The fact is, the future is already inside of them, the answers are already there, they just need a guide to help them uncover the hidden. Karen's book does just that. I love how she not only uses examples of people we all know, but then she uses her own life to help you understand yours.

If indeed the one thing that sets millionaires apart from others is the fact that they read over 52 books a year, then this one must be part of the 52. I would love to have her as a guest on my Loving Life TV Show and help get this message out to a hurting world.

Dr. Tim Weir

Karen Flaherty "knocked it out of the park" with this book! She has taken the mystery out of Human Design. Using Karen's 12 Principles, you will learn how to be mindful and notice your life transform.

Inez Bracy, PhD
Inez Bracy International

"Life these days can get busy, so busy, such that we forget who we are and lose sight of our unique strengths. Karen's work with Human Design is designed to help you re-focus and this guidebook is ideal for helping you move from intention and ideas to action. Get this book and get started today!"

Camille Leon
Founder, The Holistic Chamber of Commerce

"Getting to Know YOU"
Bonus Page

To receive a complimentary mp3 of the audiobook, please visit:
Https://LivingbyHumanDesign.com/gtkyaudio/

*

To receive a complimentary Human Design chart, please visit:
Https://LivingbyHumanDesign.com/gtkychart/
It will help you to follow along in the book much more easily, if you
have your own Human Design chart with you as you read.

DEDICATION

To my wonderfully supportive, generous, and brilliant husband,
who has lovingly kept me grounded for the past twenty-five years.
You've been the string beneath my balloon!

TABLE OF CONTENTS

Foreword

PREFACE

Chapter 1 Introduction to Human Design

Chapter 2 Your Relationships

Chapter 3 Your Health

Chapter 4 Parenting Your Children

Chapter 5 Your Career

Chapter 6 Your Spirituality

Chapter 7 Next Steps on Your Path

Testimonials

RESOURCES

ABOUT THE AUTHOR

ACKNOWLEDGMENTS

Foreword

My Human Design analysis with Karen in 2011 changed my life. She was a godsend, a blessing, and an answer to a prayer I had all that year—that I wanted to get to know myself better. I wanted to understand myself and know more about myself spiritually. I had taken many personality tests and profiles before, and while learning something from each of them, I still felt that something was missing: information about my soul. The combination of spiritual and personal features provided in the Human Design reading I got from Karen gave me more profound insight into, and a more detailed description of, who I am and why I'm here.

Karen is perfect for Human Design work, being the non-judgmental, kind, caring, and intelligent woman that she is. Her desire and abilities to help others is profound, and she has some of the warmest communication skills I've ever encountered. She took the time and patience to explain everything very clearly to me—often more than once. There were some new concepts for me to try to understand, and her calm nature, caring intentions, and soothing voice paved the way for me to learn them. Karen told me some very personal information and did so with gentleness and discretion. I was able to hear things about myself that I used to think were weird or embarrassing but learned from her that they were just part of my Human Design. Whenever I hear Karen's voice on the phone, I know that there is love in this world.

That's why I'm thrilled that Karen has written this book and that you are interested in learning more about what Human Design is and what it can do for you.

Here are some examples of what I learned and how Human Design helped me love and accept myself on an even deeper level.

Back in 2011: Karen informed me that I was a "Manifestor" and that this was rare (eight percent of population). At first I thought,

"So what, doesn't everyone have ideas?" And then she explained the depth, breadth, and frequency of manifesting that I was capable of and it hit home. No wonder I hadn't met many people like me and I felt freakish! It was a great relief to know how I was special.

The analysis revealed that I was not using my power fully and it matched with a deep level of dissatisfaction I was having with myself. When Karen told me this, I cried. It released a fear I had of somehow being "wrong" in the world because of my uniqueness and desire to make things happen (all the time! I can't shut it off). People accused me of being a control freak, but I always saw it as just wanting to make things better (according to me, of course) and doing everything I could to produce a positive outcome. I couldn't help it if I kept getting ideas for solving problems.

My Human Design reading explained to me why and how things work out for me: When my intentions are strong and there is a clear spiritual path for a great outcome, it happens. Ideas come to me, words come to me, resources come to me. This works for me individually, in projects with others, and with my spouse. My wife and I are a powerhouse when we work on a goal together, and I understood this dynamic better after we had a couples reading. She's a "Generator," someone who gets things done. And that's an understatement! I ended up appreciating my wife more because of these insights, and now she's also a very big fan of Human Design.

Being identified as a Manifestor changed my life and my image of myself. It brought me to a deeper level of self-acceptance and raised my self-esteem profoundly. I could no longer tell myself that there was something wrong with me for having so many goals, projects, or ideas that I wanted to accomplish. That's just the way I was made and why I am here.

Fast forward to 2018: The main part of the reading (my type is Manifestor) has stayed with me for seven years now, and it feels like a natural part of me and the basis for my understanding of who I am. Other parts of the reading have come up as important over the years and given me insight and understanding about why I behave or react in certain ways. I used to interpret my wife's "suggestions" for what to do as pressure to do them quickly, but they are not. I need to relax and take a deep breath and not react negatively or push back. This information helps me be more patient with my wife. It was highly valuable when she was ill and needed help, which I had to learn was not a big pressure on me, just an opportunity to be loving and supportive in different ways. My Human Design reading could well have saved our relationship.

What happened in my life as a result? I like myself more. I accept my quirks, "ways," and abilities more. I can say "I am enough" and feel that it is true. I came here with certain qualities, all the ones I need to fulfill my chart/destiny. I accept that I am a writer, a teacher, a healer in my own way. Despite times of fear, frustration, and self-doubt, I wrote and published my first book. I knew I could do it because I am a Manifestor, and I felt the power and energy of the Universe with me while I was writing it, so I knew it was something I was here to do.

One of my new projects is to help start a movement—the Mindfulness Matters Movement—in the government of Canada with some colleagues. We're all public servants who want to improve mental health and well-being in the workplace, and we've already been recognized as a "best practice" in the workplace after only eight months in existence. We are a grassroots movement offering public servants a place to learn more about mindfulness, resilience, and being compassionate with themselves. It's an awesome undertaking, and I have the confidence that my Manifestor energy can help it be a success when I listen to my ideas and intuition.

If I did not know my Human Design, I probably would have thought, as I once did, that "someone else could probably do a better job with that idea. I don't need to do it," or "I don't have what it takes to make this project happen." There's a big change in me to take a chance on such a meaningful project.

On the relationship front, it's been extremely helpful and something I am relying on to help us. My wife and I are both in the midst of perimenopause and other fun stuff, and we get annoyed at each other (and everything else in life) easily. Our Human Design couples reading told us that closeness and intimacy came easily and naturally to us and that our challenge was balancing with enough separation. All that easy intimacy is going wild during perimenopause—there seems to be too much of the closeness dynamic, making the annoyance more intense. Our challenge to get enough separation and balance is therefore greater because it's not our default way of connecting, but we understand what's going on and that helps ENORMOUSLY. Thanks to the information that Karen's reading empowered us with, we know that our Human Designs are having a new adventure together!

By far the best gift Karen's reading gave me was the gift of inner peace! I now have a better sense of who I am, why I'm here, and I know that there is nothing wrong with me. I am able to embrace myself more than ever before. Karen's work was so incredibly helpful on a deep, soul-filled level that I cannot thank her enough for the gift of my intensive Human Design reading. It really is a gift that keeps on giving.

I highly recommend working with Karen and doing a Human Design analysis of yourself and your loved ones. I hope you will enjoy treating yourself to the rich results of this fun, genuinely effective, and life-changing analysis.

Karen - Congratulations on this book, your courage, and talent!

Love and big blessings,

Jill Abramczyk
B.Soc.Sc., LL.B., M.S.W.
Author of *It Gets Better Now! A Tool Guide for Teens*

PREFACE

Is This the Book you're looking for??

Life is a series of choices. Big choices, little choices. Easy choices, hard choices. Happy choices, sad choices. What to wear, what to eat, what to do, where to go. Choices about school, work, where to live, who to love, kids, parents, vacations, and retirement. Some with really big consequences; others not so much.

I realize that reading or even buying this book is a choice, and I want you to choose correctly for you. Because, in fact, this is a book about the choices you make in your life.

So here's what you can expect right now: I'm going to let you know what the book's about, who it's written for, why you may need to know this, why it may be relevant to you now, and how it might make your life better.

What This Book is About

"Getting to Know YOU" is about getting from Point A to Point B in your life without fear. Most people go through life, as I used to, bumbling from one decision to another. And not getting what they want. Or if they don't bumble—if they're absolutely sure about their decision—they still wonder why they're not getting what they really want out of life. Either way—making clueless or rock-solid decisions—they're still unhappy.

Human Design has been around for just over thirty years now—since 1987—and yet only a small percentage of people on the planet know about it. This book sets out to make Human Design, and the concepts behind it, more user-friendly for many. For me, Human Design was the answer to my bumbling decision-making. And I'm so glad that I found it. You may be, too. We're not perfect, and many of us are just bumbling along in default mode. In fact, you may have heard others use the term "perfectly imperfect." That's your life; that's my life. We're all here to do the best we can with the tools we have in the place we're planted at the moment. But I have found that Human Design can make the ride a lot smoother than previously imagined!

(Note: if you're happy *and* getting everything you want in life, then you've figured it all out and don't need this book! Please give it to someone who does need it. Thanks!)

Is this YOU?

What is life like when it's hard to make decisions and each time you do make a decision, you worry about the outcome? This is what it can look like:

- Are you **miserable** because you're moving from one job to the next without a clear path for your future?

- Are you **unhappy** in relationships when you know there's more that you want?

- Are you **frustrated** because you realize your kids are growing up and you're growing apart? OR they're not claiming their independence at all?

- Are you feeling **let down** because you're expecting others to make you happy?

- Are you so **stressed** at work that it's hard to get anything done? And you feel so drained you don't care?

If any of these situations resonate with you, then you're in the right place. But also if you're curious, if you're always investigating new ways to get information about yourself, if you're a spiritual seeker, *or* if you've taken every class and read every book about your particularly challenging situation and are still looking for the answer. And you may have even had a Human Design reading at some time in the past but didn't quite get it at that time or you weren't ready for the information yet. You're absolutely in the right place.

Why You'll Want to Read this Book

Using a newish personality assessment tool called Human Design, you'll gain an awareness about yourself that takes away a lot of the doubt, suspicion, fear, anxiety, and emotional drama that goes into making decisions for 99% of us. Very simply, for each of us, there *is* a Strategy for making decisions. Once you know this, and practice using it, over time, your decisions are made with decisiveness, authority, and intention. You feel proud and satisfied with each decision you make because it brings you closer to your goals. Big or small, all your choices begin to fall into place to create the life that you've been dreaming of.

I've come up with a list of the "Principles of Human Design" (below) that will help explain it a little and help you to figure out if you want to choose to read this book—or pass on it for now.

Who Am I to Make This Claim?

Since learning about Human Design in early 2009, I've run thousands of charts, done hundreds and hundreds of Human Design sessions with my clients—individuals, couples, families, and business people—spoken at dozens of venues, presented Human Design at loads of holistic fairs, and studied relentlessly to understand Human Design logically. It had to be logical for me. That's who I am—a geek who doesn't really trust other people to come up with new ways of doing things, unless I can prove that it works. And I wasn't going to risk my reputation for something that was considered "too out there" by business associates, friends, and family. (They still think I'm weird, but less than they used to.)

I should add that before I learned about my Human Design chart and how to make decisions, I was a classic bumbler. For the first fifty-two years of my life, I *never* trusted my decisions. I always felt like I was flying by the seat of my pants and the sky was about to crash in. I went to school, worked in Corporate America for over thirty years, got married, and did all the things you're supposed to do. I made a lot of decisions. Now, they weren't all bad decisions—some of them turned out just fine. Some even remarkably well—like saying "yes" to my husband of twenty-five years. But I never, ever trusted my decisions at the time I was making them. And that's where finding out about my Human Design made all the difference. I could stop worrying, stop being a nervous wreck, and stop beating myself up when I made the wrong decision. And eventually learn how to live in the moment. It was a huge change in my life—and in my peace of mind.

That's what I intend for you to get out of this book, too. And this is just *my* perspective of Human Design. You may find it different from others or you may find it similar. Simplifying Human Design a bit and getting rid of a lot of the jargon worked for me. I hope it works for you, too.

Why Should You Care?

Because *I* care. No, I don't know you personally, but I know hundreds and hundreds of clients just like you who have benefited from hearing about their Human Design and using their Strategy to make decisions without fear. Here are some of the things they have to say:

"I could not believe how accurate the session was about how I work, so to speak, going over my chart in great depth to help me understand myself. I believe everyone should have a Human Design reading to help fully understand yourself. It's all there in your own unique blueprint; your strengths, weaknesses, patterns, thoughts. It was a truly amazing gift to one's self, and I highly recommend it."

"Thank you so much for last night. I'm still blown away! I feel so good today, a huge sense of relief and a massive pressure I've released from myself. I can say I'm starting to feel more like myself (I know it sounds so silly, but I know you understand.) and trusting that and releasing the doubts I held around aspects of myself. So many people's projections of me can just bugger off now! Ha-ha! Still a lot to work on, but I feel so positive with the awareness I now have and what more I will develop to absolutely improve the quality of my life. YAY!! Thank you so much for what you do and allowing us to find confidence in exactly who we are."

"I knew our sessions would be interesting, but I had no idea of the impact they would have on my everyday life. The information is in a very easy to understand format so that you can go back and reference what was discussed . . . walks you through step by step in how the information she is giving you can be applied to make the most of your life. We ended up doing my husband's and our child's as well. It without a doubt strengthened my marriage and made for a more harmonious family life. I learned some of the reasons my husband does what he does is because of his Human Design. We also have a child with special needs who is pre-verbal—having the tool for understanding his Human Design has helped me understand him better and how to pick and choose my battles when parenting. It gave me so much confidence in decision-making."

My Promise to YOU

Human Design is about self-awareness: getting to know yourself better so you can be happier, healthier, more prosperous, and more fulfilled. Things should flow easily when you're living your design. There's no pushing hard when you're in the flow of your own decision-making process.

So is This For Me?

Please take a look at the Principles below and then, if and only if, they resonate with you, please join me on a journey to find a new awareness of you that's been hidden for far too long. If it feels right for you, please don't wait any longer to find out who you really are and make decisions that feel right for you. Enjoy!

The Principles of Human Design

1. You are a unique being. The combination of who you are and why you are here is as unique as your fingerprints.

2. It's much *easier* to be who you really are than who you think you *should* be.

3. You are who you are, and nothing can change that. You're beautiful just as you are.

4. Human Design helps you remember who you are. You were born perfectly and nothing has changed.

5. Human Design is about making decisions that are right for you versus what's right for anyone else.

6. You don't need to be fixed. You're perfect just the way you are.

7. You're here for a reason. The world is waiting for the authentic you to emerge.

8. Human Design allows you to be the *you* you were born to be. You don't need to take anything personally; it's just energy.

9. If each one of us were living our unique Strategy, the world would be a lovely and very livable place.

10. You are designed to receive love and everything you need to survive. The Universe is always taking care of you by default, if you allow It.

11. Human Design is about self-awareness: getting to know yourself better so you can be happier, healthier, more prosperous, and more fulfilled.

12. Things should flow easily when you're living your design. There's no pushing hard when you're in the flow. Relationships, job offers, money, and fulfillment will flow to you and through you naturally.

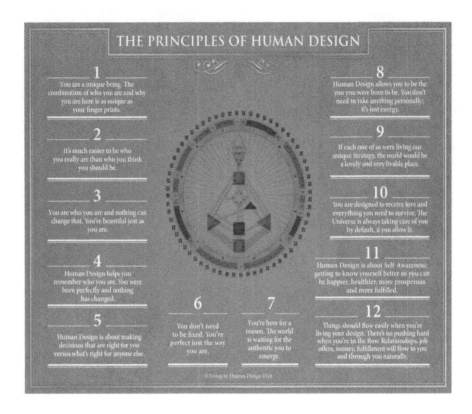

THE PRINCIPLES OF HUMAN DESIGN

1
You are a unique being. The combination of who you are and why you are here is as unique as your finger prints.

2
It's much easier to be who you really are than who you think you should be.

3
You are who you are and nothing can change that. You're beautiful just as you are.

4
Human Design helps you remember who you are. You were born perfectly and nothing has changed.

5
Human Design is about making decisions that are right for you versus what's right for anyone else.

6
You don't need to be fixed. You're perfect just the way you are.

7
You're here for a reason. The world is waiting for the authentic you to emerge.

8
Human Design allows you to be the you you were born to be. You don't need to take anything personally; it's just energy.

9
If each one of us were living our unique Strategy, the world would be a lovely and very livable place.

10
You are designed to receive love and everything you need to survive. The Universe is always taking care of you by default, if you allow it.

11
Human Design is about Self-Awareness; getting to know yourself better so you can be happier, healthier, more prosperous and more fulfilled.

12
Things should flow easily when you're living your design. There's no pushing hard when you're in the flow. Relationships, job offers, money, fulfillment will flow to you and through you naturally.

© Living by Human Design 2018

Link to complementary audio book download:
https://LivingbyHumanDesign.com/gtkyaudio/

Chapter 1
Introduction to Human Design

What is Human Design?

"This knowledge is not about changing anything. And it's not about changing anyone . . . Human Design is not a dogma. It's a matrix. It's only a formula. It's not moralistic. There is no good or bad. There is no good design and bad design. It doesn't exist. There is truly nothing but the revealed beauty of what each of us is." ~Ra Uru Hu, transcribed from the "How to Read Your Chart" lecture, given in Sedona, AZ, on August 28, 1999. *Permission for each quote from Ra granted by Chaitanyo of The Human Design System, based in New Mexico, who made the original recordings of Ra's US seminars from 1993-2000.*

Everyone was on edge. Aunt Mary's evening shift was especially worrisome during the riots in the Summer of 1967. Everyone begged her not to go to work each day as the riots escalated. But each day, Aunt Mary and her colleague at the paper, Clarence, would ride down together right into and through the heart of the violence. The paper reported it, but they were in the thick of it to deliver the news. We would look for our paper each morning to see the news, and when it got really bad it was even on TV. If the New York channels thought it was bad enough to make the news alongside the Vietnam War and the political scene, then it must be bad!

I'm old enough (just barely) to remember the civil rights movements of the '60s, the anti-war protests and assassinations of 1968, Kent State in 1970, and the violent political conventions in 1968. The spillover effect of those events affected cities all across the country, including Newark, NJ, not far from where we were living. My Aunt Mary lived in Maplewood with my grandmother and worked at the Newark Star-Ledger as a typesetter. (For my younger readers, a typesetter–believe it or not–was someone who put little metal block letters side by side to create the news articles in lines and columns for each page of the newspaper to be printed. It's a profession long gone now, but it was important for hundreds of years. We thought it was pretty cool when we got to visit the paper!)

Grandma was still working the day shift at a button factory in Harrison, adjacent to Newark; Uncle Johnny was a biology teacher at Central High School in Newark, but they were out for the summer; and Aunt Mary worked the night shift (3pm–midnight) at the paper because that's when the papers were printed.

I was eleven that summer and wasn't sure what to make of it. Everyone seemed to be walking on eggshells. Unfortunately for me, I had a really bad case of poison sumac just during this period, so I was laid up on the couch watching too much TV—feeling miserable but with an unusual vantage point as everyone else was out playing. The muted reactions of my parents were enough to make me wonder how and why this could be happening in the peaceful Garden State during the summer. But the only question I heard each morning as my mother called my grandmother was, "Did Aunt Mary make it home safely?"

We might long sometimes for the innocence and sweetness of the past, but I'm here to remind you that the Summer of 1967 was anything but innocent and sweet. (Ironically, it's now referred to nostalgically as the "Summer of Love" because of the San Francisco love-ins.) It was most likely the summer when I realized—and many of my friends and family realized—there really was anger and hatred and violence in a world where I had mostly been isolated. Of course, I fought with my brothers and sisters, my parents believed in corporal punishment (as many parents did at that time), and there was a war a half-world away. But this felt different. I guess it was my coming-of-age summer.

It took a very long time to feel safe driving into Newark by myself—and many people still recommended against it even years later.

So now it feels like we're revisiting the past. We've grown up, matured, and have hopefully become less fearful of each other.

I wonder: Is it okay now to love rather than blame? To talk rather than shoot? To explain rather than shout? To understand rather than condemn?
I hope so. I pray so. I intend and imagine and envision so.

*****

First off, congratulations on deciding to read this book, to discover your unique Strategy for making decisions that you're confident about, and to learn more about Human Design in general. While this is a very high-level discussion of Human Design, you'll be able to learn a lot about your own personal chart as you listen to the stories and figure out which pieces apply to you and your chart—and which don't! Once again, here are the Principles I mentioned in the Preface. These Principles of Human Design help to set the stage:

The Principles of Human Design

1. You are a unique being. The combination of who you are and why you are here is as unique as your fingerprints.

2. It's much easier to be who you really are than who you think you should be.

3. You are who you are, and nothing can change that. You're beautiful just as you are.

4. Human Design helps you remember who you are. You were born perfect and nothing has changed.

5. Human Design is about making decisions that are right for you versus what's right for anyone else.

6. You don't need to be fixed. You're perfect just the way you are.

7. You're here for a reason. The world is waiting for the authentic you to emerge.

8. Human Design allows you to be the you you were born to be. You don't need to take anything personally; it's just energy.

9. If each one of us were living our unique Strategy, the world would be a lovely and very livable place.

10. You are designed to receive love and everything you need to survive. The Universe is always taking care of you by default, if you allow It.

11. Human Design is about self-awareness: getting to know yourself better so you can be happier, healthier, more prosperous, and more fulfilled.

12. Things should flow easily when you're living your design. There's no pushing hard when you're in the flow. Relationships, job offers, money, fulfillment will flow to you and through you naturally.

Note: If you would like to get your own Human Design chart, you can get a complimentary chart here:
Https://LivingbyHumanDesign.com/GTKYchart/

The premise of this book is that making choices for a lot of us can be difficult. It can make us fearful, it can create triggers that have us relive past mistakes, it can create anxiety and sometimes even make us physically sick.

Making a big decision requires a certain amount of self-awareness, would you agree? If we don't have clarity about what we want, who we are in this situation, and what the consequences may be, how can we make a good decision? Please notice that I didn't say rational decision. As it turns out, ninety-two percent of us shouldn't be using our heads at all to make decisions. This will sound odd to many, and I don't blame you one bit. I always made decisions from my head. How else could you figure out the pros and cons of a situation? Human Design looks at that a little differently—but more about that later.

Self-awareness of ourselves is what allows us to assess a situation. When we don't have self-awareness—or at least enough to feel comfortable making a decision in a specific situation—we get fearful or even put ourselves in victim mode. We wonder if we're doing the right thing. We question ourselves throughout the process. And afterward, we second-guess our decision until we know for sure how it's turned out—for better or worse.

This book will lay out the solutions to self-awareness that Human Design affords, allowing us to make decisions that feel good and are good for us, while dispelling the fears and anxieties normally associated with decision-making. As we go through chapter by chapter, I'll lay out how making better decisions can help in the areas of our life that cause the most trouble: Relationships, Health, Parenting, Career, and Spirituality; what are the most common issues for each category; and then how Human Design can help you make better choices.

But first, let's dive a little deeper into what Human Design is and lay out the Energy Centers and Energy Types. Then, as the chapters progress, we'll discuss some of Human Design's basic premises about energy vibrations, consciousness, conditioning and the Law of Attraction.

What is Human Design?

Human Design is still kind of new in the realm of personality assessment tools. It was created in 1987, so only a little over thirty years ago, by Ra Uru Hu, formerly known as the Canadian businessman, Robert Krakower. Officially, Ra considered himself the "Founder and Messenger of the Human Design System." You've probably heard of other personality tools, like Myers-Briggs or DISC or Enneagram or the Big Five? This one is quite a bit different for a few reasons:

1. It will give you a new way of looking at yourself—not just as you read this, but for the rest of your life.

2. Human Design is based on your birth information—time, date, and location. It's not based on a bunch of questions that you subjectively answer. It's an objective mathematical equation based upon your birth information. Therefore, it's very specific to you and tells you a lot about yourself, such as traits, preferences, ways of learning and being in relationships, and a lot more.

3. Human Design is based on a synthesis of a number of ancient wisdoms—including the Chinese I'Ching, the Judaic Kabbalah, the Hindu Chakra system, and Eastern and Western astrologies—along with the modern sciences: quantum physics, modern math, and biogenetics. Putting those all together, it's a very potent mix of these sciences. In the past, the ancient wisdoms worked well and were used for thousands of years. On the modern side, the sciences are actually just catching up with Human Design to explain how our bodies work in terms of energy, vibrations, and interactions with others. For example, Ra Uru Hu said in 1987 that neutrinos had mass; it wasn't until 1994 that scientists discovered the same thing.

4. Human Design as a personality tool is cutting edge because it gives you so much information, so many insights and awareness into you—your personality traits, your Strategy for making decisions, ways of being, how you get into and out of relationships, jobs, etc., your learning style, and so much more.

5. It's accurate, insightful, and very specific. Guaranteed: It's way more information than you've ever heard about yourself from one source.

What Human Design tells you is what's right for you. Nobody else—just you. With all the sciences coming together, it creates a powerful, but very practical system of knowledge that can be used by you every day of your life—if you choose to use it.

That's what I like about Human Design: Whether you're having a full session about your chart or you've just heard about your type and Strategy very briefly from someone like me for a few minutes at a holistic fair, you can be assured that your life will change, if you choose to use the information. (It's always up to you, of course!) It might change a little, it might change a lot, or it might save your life because you've been living with the pain of not knowing who you really are for so long. It's that powerful! And I know it will change your life, too, just as it's changed mine.

A lot of times, I talk with people who have already figured out their Strategy and use it sometimes. When they use their Strategy, they nail the decision process they're going through. And other times, they don't use it and wonder why their results are different. It's because they didn't use their Strategy consistently. Instead, they used their head to figure out the pros and cons or they listened to someone else's opinion of what would be "right" for them. But once you know what your Strategy is, and you realize that you can count on it consistently, it's reassuring. It becomes your go-to Strategy, and after a while, no one will dissuade you from using it—ever.

For example, if your Energy Type happens to be a Generator or Manifesting Generator, then you might have already figured out that you should be following your gut to make decisions. There were probably times in your life when you didn't follow your gut, and then later on, said to yourself, "Oh, gosh, I wish I had followed my gut on that one!" And then there were other times, when you did follow your gut and you think "Oh, yeah, nailed it!" and it feels good, too. If you think you have figured out what your Strategy is, I'm here to confirm that for you. I'm here to give you some peace around what works for you and what doesn't. And if you're still figuring out what your Strategy is, I'll lay out the Strategy and give you the instructions on how to make it work in your life.

Human Design is really about making the decisions that are right for you and not making the decisions that everyone else thought you should make. Everyone in your life—parents, teachers, friends, spouse, relatives—they're all well-meaning. I won't take that away from anyone. They all had your best interests at heart—at least ninety-nine percent of them, I would guess. But they don't know you and what's best for you, according to your Human Design chart. And how could they?

So now it's time to do what's right for you—nobody else—just you! Because you were perfect when you were born and that's what your chart shows—the moment you were born. If we had been allowed to follow our divine design from the moment we were born—and believe me, none of us were allowed to do that thirty, forty, or fifty years ago—things would have turned out quite differently for most of us. That's all water under the bridge. We don't have to worry about that anymore. But now we get to move forward. Let's use what we know now. Let's love you, let's love this chart, take it all forward, and do the best we can with the brilliance of the chart you've been given.

And it still won't be the perfect life, but it will be much more life-affirming for you. It will be life-confirming. It will bring you reassurance, inner peace, and you'll be able to sleep better at night knowing that you're living the best life for you. That you're doing the best you can with what you've got in your toolkit—and now you know you've got a good toolkit, a great toolkit. You're capable, you're strong, you're a survivor—and it's all there in your chart. And there's nothing that can take that away from you.

Some Benefits of Human Design

Human Design is a pragmatic system to understand yourself and find inner peace through self-awareness. With the knowledge you'll gain through understanding your unique Human Design, you'll be able to solve any issues or challenges that come your way in life.
Here are some of the benefits that my clients and I have found from discovering their Human Design:

First of all, it gives you a better understanding of yourself. You're going to know you pretty intimately by the time you've learned what there is to discover from your chart.

Then what happens after you know and love yourself is that you find that it's a lot easier to understand other people who are important to you. How are you alike? How are you different? All the similarities and differences become much more apparent, and all of a sudden, they're not such a big deal. They're just what is. And it's okay. You get to be more accepting of both yourself and others. You get to understand your spouse and relatives better, your children better, your colleagues better. They're not relationship-ending differences anymore, or conflict-inducing, or even worthy of a discussion (for the most part). How did that happen? (Hint: with very little effort on your part.) It's just awareness.

Human Design will also help you to discover your gifts and talents. The traits that you thought were you, consistently, will be confirmed. And the things that you weren't so sure about or that showed up more inconsistently—those will be confirmed also. And that's okay. All of a sudden you get to let go of the inconsistent traits—because they're not the consistent you. And that's okay. So if you don't have willpower—for example, sixty-seven percent of us don't—you don't have to make believe you do, or wish you had it, or take another course to get it! And you can let go of all the thoughts that occupy your mind about it. That will free up a lot of space in your head, believe me!

So what your chart does is reassure and confirm for you who you are and allows you to let go of who you aren't! There's plenty of stuff that other people get to do that you don't necessarily have to do and you don't care to do. It doesn't matter to you. Let them do it. I don't know about you, but in my head, there were a lot of things taking up room about what I thought I should be doing.

Human Design will provide an accurate and reliable decision-making and action-taking Strategy that works with your Energy Type. Always. Not sometimes, but always and in any situation. Many of us try to make it more complicated, but the simplicity of each Strategy is elegant and belies the significance of how it can change your life.

Finally, there will be some traits in your chart that you may think of as "weaknesses." But these come in lots of shapes and sizes, and what I find is that they're always there to teach us an invaluable lesson and send us on our journey to more peace and fulfillment than we could have imagined. If you don't have willpower in your chart, that's okay. You're here to have a different kind of wisdom when it comes to willpower. (More on that later!) Those traits that we think of as "weaknesses" are a lesson for us!

THE ENERGY CENTERS

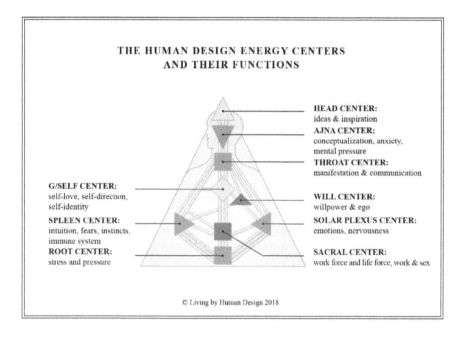

**THE HUMAN DESIGN ENERGY CENTERS
AND THEIR FUNCTIONS**

HEAD CENTER:
ideas & inspiration

AJNA CENTER:
conceptualization, anxiety, mental pressure

THROAT CENTER:
manifestation & communication

G/SELF CENTER:
self-love, self-direction, self-identity

SPLEEN CENTER:
intuition, fears, instincts, immune system

ROOT CENTER:
stress and pressure

WILL CENTER:
willpower & ego

SOLAR PLEXUS CENTER:
emotions, nervousness

SACRAL CENTER:
work force and life force, work & sex

© Living by Human Design 2018

Now, if you have your chart in hand, let's talk about the Energy Centers you can see on it. These are the nine geometric shapes on the chart. They generally follow the pattern of the Hindu Chakra system, with a few additions. We call them Energy Centers because each one carries a different type of energetic vibration. You may have heard of the word "aura." An aura around someone's body refers to the full body's energy. The nine Energy Centers are unique and carry their own energy vibration. A way to think about this is if you went to the hospital and had two tests: an EKG and an EEG on the same day. The EKG is for your heart, and the EEG is for your brain. If you compared the two tests (which both read out as a graph with ups and downs), you would notice that they looked different from each other. They each carry their own vibration. That's what we're saying for all the Energy Centers. They're all vibrating a little differently from each other, and together they make us the unique energy individuals that we are.

So I'll go through the body graph from top to bottom, and tell you what they're called, where they're located, and what their function is.

At the very top is the Head Center, which is the triangle pointing up. This is the center for ideas and inspiration. This is yellow if it's colored in.
Below the Head, the triangle pointing down, is called the Ajna. This is basically the Brain; some people refer to it as the Third Eye. It also handles opinions, data processing and storage, trivia, analysis, conceptualization, memories, and lots more. If it's colored in, it's green.

Just below the Ajna is the Throat, which is a square (brown if colored in). The Throat, as you might imagine, is all about creating and speaking, communication, and manifestation.

Below the Throat is the G Center, which is the large diamond in the middle of the chart. It's the center for the Self: self-love, self-identity, and self-direction. It will be yellow if it's colored in.

Then off to the right of the G is a little triangle called the Will Center. If it's colored in, it's red. The Will Center is all about willpower, ego, self-worth, and money. (Some people refer to this center as the Heart. I like to think that we all have a heart, but we don't all have willpower.)
Further to the right of the Will is the Solar Plexus, the triangle on the right side of the body graph. Brown, if it's colored in. This is the center for our emotions. It's also referred to as the Emotional Solar Plexus.

On the opposite side of the body graph is another triangle, the Spleen. Brown, if it's colored in on your chart. The Spleen covers a number of energies: intuition, fears, survival, health, and timing.

Near the bottom of the chart are two squares. The second from the bottom is the Sacral. This would be red if colored in. The Sacral is the energy for work force and life force on the planet; otherwise known as work and sex.

Lastly, at the bottom of the body graph is the Root Center, which is brown if colored in. The Root is the center for adrenaline, pressure, and stress.

The configuration of the centers that are colored in on your chart and the ones that aren't is your unique energy blueprint. So what's the difference between the white centers and the ones that are colored in?

The colored ones are called defined centers. They get to be defined when they have a line that connects one to another—kind of like a pinball machine. When there's a line, or road, colored in between two Energy Centers—in either black, red, or both red and black— then the centers on both ends of the line are lit up or defined. That's what creates definition in our chart—the lines and the centers.

In the defined centers (whether there are two or nine on your chart), you have a consistent way of processing and expressing that type of energy. It's very specific to you—it's the blueprint of your energy. When you walk into a room, this is the energy that people feel from you. Each of your defined centers are acting like radio-signal transmitters. They are literally sending out the energy of each defined center into the room, and other people are feeling those centers when theirs are *not* defined. This is what other people feel, whether it's your inspiration, your emotions, or your fears, or your grounded-ness, or your voice, for example. And these centers are not conditioned by others, like family or friends. They are consistent and stay that way all your life. When you look at your chart and see which centers are defined—that's your definition—and then realize exactly what they are, it should feel very comfortable for you. You'll probably have the reaction of "Ahhh! Yes, that's what it feels like to be me!" It should feel like coming home and realizing you were there all along.

Here's what each of the defined (colored-in) Energy Centers on your chart will generally feel like:

Energy Center	What it feels like as consistent energy
Head	You're inspiring to other people; an inspiration
Ajna	You've got a good head for details, data, memories, trivia, traditional learning style
Throat	Your voice can be heard easily (sometimes quite loudly)
G	You have a good sense of your direction in life and feel lovable
Will (also called Ego or Heart) (Motor)	You're willful, have willpower, can be egotistical
Solar Plexus (Motor)	You have an emotional wave that goes up and down between joy and melancholy on a cyclical basis
Spleen	You're intuitive, good sense of timing, usually very healthy
Sacral (Motor)	You've got a lot of energy - Energizer Bunny usually
Root (Motor)	You're grounded, rooted, dependable

The centers that are white on your chart are your open centers. When you have an open center, that means that you DON'T have a consistent way of processing that kind of energy. The open centers get influenced by the environment and whoever is around you with those centers colored in or defined. The open centers are acting like radio satellite receivers, where they are literally taking in the energy around you and then amplifying it. In the early part of our lives, these are the centers where we take in energy and think that it is *our* energy, such as the Will Center. We take it in and amplify it while that Will Center parent or teacher is around us, and think that we can do anything. Then they walk away, and we wonder where the willpower went! It's that changeable.

them a wonderful ability to converse with anyone, and their Sacral will always be open.

The Manifestor's Strategy for making decisions is to inform others before they take action. They will usually have an idea in their head (They are the only type that uses their head to make a decision.), decide whether to do it or not, and then let the people know—who have to know—what they will be doing. This creates an environment where the others can either help the Manifestor or get out of their way. Once the Manifestor decides to do something, there's usually very little chance they will be stopped. They're kind of like a speeding train going down the tracks and not stopping at any stations. They can be quite single-minded when they're in the middle of a project and may feel like any questions are a huge distraction. And if they don't take those relatively simple steps to let others know about their plans, then the Manifestor will become angry, or those affected will become angry with them—or both. Some famous Manifestors include Robert De Niro, Al Pacino, Jennifer Aniston, Pope Francis I, Paul McCartney, Maya Angelou, and George W. Bush.

Next, we have the Generators and Manifesting Generators. They are the worker bees on the planet and are seventy percent of the population—about half of each. They keep the planet buzzing with activity! In the last century, Generators and Manifesting Generators were the farmers, factory workers, and laborers who built their countries into what they are today. They would work long days, come home to take care of the family, fall into bed, and get up the next day to do it all again—usually for forty or fifty years. Now, we are fortunate to have more options. We can *choose* which career to pursue. We don't have to do the "family business" generation after generation—whatever that was. Sometimes we might forget that it was only fifty years ago when that was the case for many families. Having that choice makes all the difference.

What makes Generators and Manifesting Generators similar to one another is their defined Sacral Center. This is the big red square near the bottom of the chart. That is the largest Motor in the Human

Design chart and generally keeps them going and going and going until the day they die. They're like Energizer Bunnies—unless they've fallen ill, and sometimes even then! What makes them different is that all Manifesting Generators have a defined and motorized Throat like the Manifestors—and the Generators don't have that. Generators may have their Throat defined or open, but it is never connected to a Motor. It's the motorized connection that gives Manifesting Generators (MG's) a voice that can be heard easily.

People want to talk with them because they understand that MG's are easy to talk with, can make referrals and introductions, can be the life of the party, and (generally) are having a good time. Of course, this is a description of the MG who is generally using their Strategy to make decisions that are good for them. For Generators, it's a bit harder to be heard, especially with strangers or in an unfamiliar situation. They tend to be quieter but can also be shy or very chatty at different times. (We'll talk about the strategies for overcoming the Throat challenges in Chapter 5.)

The decision-making Strategy for Generators and Manifesting Generators is to "wait to respond." As soon as I say this, many clients are surprised and want to push back. The usual response is: "But I've used my head for all my decisions up to now." Exactly. This is one of those places in the book where I will gently suggest that not all of the advice we grew up with was in our best interest. Growing up with the Nike slogan of "Just DO It!" doesn't serve all of us. In fact, it only works for the Manifestors! The rest of us have to *wait*.

"Waiting to respond" refers to the Sacral response, which is in the gut. That gut response, whether it is positive or negative, is sending us a message. We can think of it as guidance. I like to think of it as an "Inner Guidance" system. This guidance system will unerringly take us in the direction that is correct for us. For Generators, it is simply to wait to respond to anything outside of themselves (that is, not their thoughts or their mind)—like an email, text, phone call, new person you've met, invitation to something, or maybe a new car passing by. Any of these situations would be something that a Generator can respond to either positively (uh-huh) or negatively (uhn-uh) and either move forward with an action or not. The forward action will also *feel* good to pursue, while the negative reaction will usually feel like you've dodged a bullet or simply decided to pass on something, such as buying a new car. For both Energy Types, if they are *not* following their Strategy, the usual default mode is frustration because things aren't working out, aren't happening fast enough, or feeling stuck with nowhere to turn.

For the Manifesting Generator (MG), the process is similar but has a few more steps. Because MG's are usually very quick to do everything—such as walking, talking, and eating—they can wait to respond to the same kinds of things outside themselves, but when they decide to do something that affects others, it helps to inform those who need to know, as a Manifestor would. Therefore, the complete decision-making Strategy for the Manifesting Generator is to wait to respond, think about whom it affects and how, then let them know about your intentions so that they can either help you or allow you to complete your actions by getting out of the way, and then act. Sounds complicated, but it's not once you've practiced it a few times.

Some famous Generators include Bill Gates, Steve Jobs, Oprah Winfrey, Albert Einstein, and John Lennon. Some famous Manifesting Generators include President Trump, Hillary Clinton, Ted Turner, Richard Branson, Keith Richards, Angelina Jolie, and Gwyneth Paltrow.

Next, we have the Projectors. Projectors are about twenty percent of the population, and they are here to be wise and to guide and direct the rest of us. They play an important role in helping the world to adapt to all its changes, especially as all the changes in technology, the environment, finances, and transportation accelerate. Projectors tend to be the teachers, professors, consultants, accountants, architects, and any other profession where people are coming to them for advice or education of some sort. Projectors are your friends or family who are always wanting to give you advice. And it's great advice. But it works best for them if they wait until they are asked to give their very sound, very *wise* advice.

In fact, the Projector Strategy is to "wait for the invitation." Waiting, in their case, refers only to the big decisions in life, like career, relationships, and where to live. When Projectors can accept their Strategy, prepare while they are waiting, and then accept or reject the invitation when they get it, they will be happy, productive, and admired by their friends and family. When Projectors don't follow their Strategy—when they're pushing to make things happen in their life, but things aren't working out—their default theme is to become bitter.

Some famous Projectors include: President Kennedy, President Obama, Barbra Streisand, Mick Jagger, Nelson Mandela, George Clooney, Denzel Washington, Ron Howard, and Brad Pitt.

Finally, we have the Reflectors. This is the rarest of the Energy Types, representing about one percent of the population. Reflectors are unique because each Energy Center is open—all nine of them. This means that they take in energy from everyone around them and amplify it. They literally take in the health of the community around them and then reflect it back to us, as if they are a mirror. If the community is "healthy," they will live a satisfied life and be fulfilled where they are.

If the community is not healthy, the Reflector will not be fulfilled and will likely want to move away to a community that feels better to them. Their decision-making Strategy is to "wait for twenty-eight days" before making a big decision so that they have time to mull it over through all the ups and downs of the month, and to discuss it with friends and family. At the end of that time, they'll have a good feel for the appropriate answer and can proceed with it. And when they are not following this Strategy, their default theme will be disappointment.

Some famous Reflectors include Richard Burton, Sandra Bullock, Scott Hamilton, and Rosalynn Carter.

Why I'm passionate about Human Design

Here's my chart:

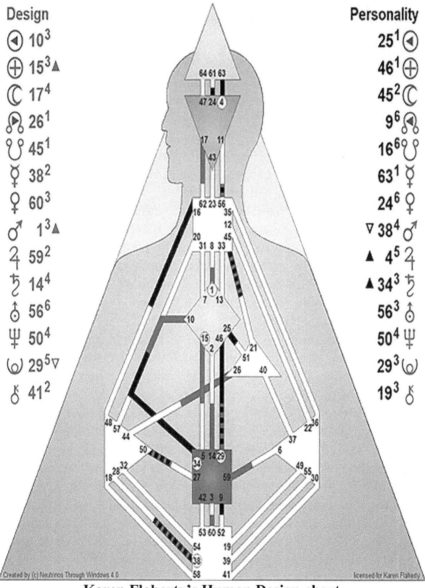

Karen Flaherty's Human Design chart

I have to say: The life I live now and the life I love now looks nothing like what I was born into and grew up with for about the first fifty years.

I got my first Human Design chart in early January of 2009 and realized there was more to me than I had realized—that I was supposed to be a teacher and a guide for others, according to my chart. I happen to be a Generator with four Energy Centers defined: the Head and Ajna, G and Sacral. Once I knew that, I started to make choices using my decision-making Strategy (which is "wait to respond"), choices that felt good, and listened to that little voice, my Inner Being, pointing me in the right direction.

I was finally able to say, "Here's who I am and here's what I want to do with my life." It took a while to get comfortable with that. Moving from Corporate America to having my own business—that was a leap. So I did it slowly but surely, with lots of ups and downs. And then I got laid off in the spring of 2014, just as we were about to move—literally the week before the house went on the market, with all the painters and electricians running around! So that was actually good news. It meant that once we settled into our new home in Florida, I could do Human Design full time.

So I had lists of intentions for each area of my life, and the Universe provided and is providing for us daily. I knew that I wanted to have my own coaching practice one day, and that day is here now. So it's a blessing for me to be able to help my clients to find out who they really are and to get past their fears, like I did. But I have to tell you that getting past the fears in my life—some from childhood, some later on—took the most time. And I'm still healing physically from some of those fears because they had such long-term detrimentally stressful effects. So that's why I've created this book—to give you a framework to think about decision-making and the fears surrounding those decisions, and to show you the awareness that's available to you along with some of the tools to use to get past the fears in a way that hopefully will save you some of the time and effort that I went through.

Now, what does this have to do with you?

Many people have benefited by knowing their Human Design and especially their Strategy for making decisions. They, like me, find that once they're in tune with who they really are and the traits they were born with, it's much simpler to be *that* person than to be someone you're not. It's exhausting to try to be the person we think we should be or were raised to be.

What are some other benefits of Human Design?

The most potent benefit is that you'll find out the characteristics and personality of the real you—the unique you that you were born to be. When you discover that unique you and begin living it day by day, you'll start to be in the flow. It's a wonderful feeling! Here are some other benefits:

- Human Design answers the questions: Who am I, and why am I here?

- It explains how we are designed and who we are as uniquely created beings.

- It shows us our specific role in the world and the track we are on with our Profile.

- It gives clear guidelines for allowing our life's purpose to flow through us.

- It tells us how to make correct decisions that point us in the correct direction of our life's purpose.

- It demonstrates how, when we operate correctly, according to our Strategy and Authority, the energy frequency of our life changes and, therefore, its outcomes change as well.

- It maps out the conditioned mind and body and reveals how we can change our earlier conditioning (conditioning that we picked up from our parents, siblings, teachers, etc.)

Tangible & Intangible Results

New Solutions to Old Problems

Being the logical person I am, after a few years of coaching and telling people about their Human Design, I wanted to see what their results really were. Were they receiving the help and getting the answers they hoped for when they sought out Human Design? So I did a survey, and it really opened my eyes to their results. They were so generous with their explanations and the real-life results they'd achieved after having a Human Design session.
Here are the questions I asked:

- What specific (tangible, if appropriate) results did you get from having a Human Design session?

- What other transformations happened in your life because of these results?

- What do you imagine would have been the cost to you had you NOT decided to have a Human Design session?

- What were the biggest sources of pain, if any, that you were eager to solve when you decided to have the session?
Some of the tangible results that clients mentioned included:

  ➢ better relationships with children/spouses
  ➢ moved into dream house near the ocean
  ➢ found fulfilling work
  ➢ started a new, thriving business
  ➢ wrote and published their first book
  ➢ liking themselves more

But just as important, or even more important for some, were the *in*tangible results, like: trusting their Inner Guidance, not second-guessing themselves, finding out who they really are, deeper levels of self-acceptance and self-esteem, and finally—the daddy of them all—inner peace.

I was so happy to hear their results and know that it had made such a profound difference in their lives. All from just a simple survey!

The bottom line is that a Human Design session can help you to demystify some of the questions in life that never seem to get resolved. It puts you in control of the cultural norms that don't seem to fit you. It makes distinctions for you that may not have occurred to you before. It gives you strategies to tackle your emotional issues—whether you're "overly" emotional or at the mercy of others' emotions. It gives you strategies for your life and your business. Overall, a Human Design session will give you new solutions to old issues. It will change your perspective on a whole lot of things!!

My Promise to You

Now that you've heard about so many of the benefits of Human Design, I must admit that it's not a slam-dunk solution to all the challenges in your life. It does require a willingness to make a change, if you decide to move forward. That's not always easy. I get it.

There are more chapters in the book that get into specifics about how Human Design can make a difference in the challenging areas of your life. No matter which area your particular challenge is in, there's still some letting go of the current situation involved. Are you ready to let that go?

Are you also ready to let go of the you that you *thought* you were when you got into this challenging situation? Maybe that's where you need to let go a bit, too.

For example, do you sometimes wish that you were taller or thinner? Who doesn't, you might ask?

Or do you wish that you had more willpower? Or that you felt more lovable or had a better sense of direction about your life? Those are fairly common "wishes"—we all have some version of a wish we'd like to have happen. But...

What if you just weren't born with that particular trait? What if you were able to know and understand, once and for all—just as you know that you won't be taller or too much thinner—that you just don't have that trait, you never will, and it's okay? Would that be okay with you?

In fact, it's actually more than okay because you were created that way for a reason. You may not know exactly what it is yet. But you were born this way so that you could live out your life's purpose in this lifetime. And you absolutely have all the traits and abilities and internal resources at your fingertips that you'll need to fulfill your life's purpose. There's no need for more because you're enough just the way you are.

In Human Design, we say that you get to be the you that you were born to be. After you find out your Energy Type and Strategy, or have a Human Design session, you're free to move about the world without the pre-conceived notions of your parents, siblings, teachers, and friends, who all meant well. Those conditioning ideas are likely what holds you back from your own authenticity. You're allowed to let them go—just let those conditioned beliefs go because they don't serve you. Do you think that you can let them go?

Are you ready to let go of the old stuff and live free?

Are you ready to let go of the person you think you are so that you can live a life of freedom, growth, and joy?

Let's get started!

I was fifty-two years old when I came upon Human Design. I wish I had known about this earlier in my life. It would have made a big difference in how I made some of my decisions and would have reassured me when I just happened to be following my Strategy without realizing it. It would have been nice to have known earlier. On the other hand, it's never too late to discover the real you. In fact, I highly recommend it, no matter how old or young you are.

Now that you know a little about Human Design and how you can use it to make decisions that you're confident of, let's delve into how it can help you in relationships with your family, friends, and colleagues.

Chapter 2
YourRelationships

Most Common Issues in Relationships

> "There is only one major dilemma in being human. And that dilemma is: 'Can I trust the decisions that I make?' I mean, there isn't anything else. There really isn't. Nothing else. It's the only real thing that human beings have to deal with. Because the moment that you can know that the decision that you have made is correct for you, that's about as weightless as you ever become. You slowly start levitating off the ground—don't take me seriously! It's an extraordinary thing. It is lightness, and it's all about knowing what a reliable decision is. If you have that within yourself, if you can trust your decision-making process, it will not matter whether you crash into a tree or you have a celebration. But you won't carry the burden of 'Oh, I shouldn't have done this!' or 'I wish I had done that.' The moment that you are clear in your decision-making process, the burden is gone."
> Ra Uru Hu, 1999.

Relationships make the world go round! Many can be very satisfying—they provide the juiciness of life! But they're not always easy. They can be downright frustrating and perplexing sometimes.

Whether it's with children, parents, a spouse, work teams, colleagues, friends, or extended family, most of us deal with other people all day every day. So let's start with relationships as a place where Human Design can play a role in making things easier, simpler, and more satisfying overall.

My clients deal with a lot of common issues:

- Communications in general
➢ What we say, how we say it, what we do and don't say, intonation, shy vs. chatty

- Handling disagreements between family members
➢ Good cop vs. bad cop at home, conflict vs. appeasement, drama for the sake of drama, intensity

- The stress of today's scheduling for parents and children
➢ Competing priorities, setting boundaries, taking "me" time vs. family time, not enough time

- The intrusion of technology at home, at work, and at school
➢ Allowing growth while keeping the peace, keeping lines of communication open, agreeing on times to limit the use of technology

- Rekindling a relationship with a spouse after the kids are grown
➢ How have you both changed over time, or have you changed? Who is this stranger?

Yes, these common issues are varied, but they all boil down to an understanding around awareness and communicating in a way that allows everyone to have their say and live their lives according to their own Human Design Strategy.

Since this is the first set of issues we're dealing with, I want to lay out a few basics. When we follow our Human Design Strategy, it's equally important to know about and practice the Law of Attraction.

You may have heard of the Law of Attraction. It's been made popular by the movie *The Secret* and by authors and teachers such as Wayne Dyer, Abraham-Hicks, Deepak Chopra, Mike Dooley, Louise Hay, and others. But it's been around for a long time. Some of the first books were in the late 1800s and early 1900s, such as *Think and Grow Rich* and *The Master Key*.

The Law of Attraction basically says that what we think about we attract into our reality. There's truth to that, but a lot of people *think* it means that their minds will bring them exactly what they want. That's only part of it. We'll get into more specifics about the Law of Attraction below and in Chapter 5, but if you're curious now, the Resources section at the end of the book will point you to some of the teachers I follow.

When I first heard about Human Design, I had been studying the Law of Attraction for almost ten years. And I was concerned that they may not be complementary disciplines. So I was very relieved to find out that not only were they complimentary, they actually knit together very well. Kind of like the whole being more than the sum of its parts.

To put this all together for relationships, let's delve further into what it means to have a decision-making Strategy, how to use the Law of Attraction with Human Design, how to be the authentic version of yourself, and how to get beyond our fears when we're making decisions. Each of these challenges play a role in dysfunctional relationships. As usual, it starts with working on ourselves a bit before we're ready for prime time!

Free Will vs. Human Design Strategy

Do you still get to do what *you* want to do? That's a question that comes up frequently during a Human Design session. Some clients wonder if using Human Design limits them, taking away their unlimited choices. If I'm following my Human Design Strategy, then what role does my free will play? Do I still have unlimited choices for what I can do, or am I limited by this new Strategy?

Of course, you will always have the unlimited choices that your consciousness can provide in any situation. But you'll always feel better and be better aligned with your own path, *if* you follow your Strategy.

A lot of times, this question seems to come from a lack of confidence or trust in the Strategy or, even worse, distrust that the Universe will provide for you. That trust comes with time, but it is also readily apparent as soon as you start practicing your Strategy.

And, besides, do you really believe that a completely unlimited world of choices is such a great thing? Most people are overwhelmed as it is with *too many* choices on a day-to-day basis. How many times are there too many paths, people, choices, or opportunities to choose from? Wouldn't it be nice if you could depend on your own internal guidance system (your Strategy) to make a decision that's correct for you?

Because that's the choice you have. Once you know about your Strategy, you will need to decide whether you should hold on to the mantra of unlimited choices where you can do anything you choose to do or if you should adhere to the *"limits"* of your Strategy and choose what's correct for you.

I don't know about you, but I've been down enough dead ends and roads to nowhere to think that doing what's *"correct"* for me might not be such a bad option. Is choosing to do what's correct for you really such a hardship when it's usually the very thing that will lead you on a path that's correct for your health, prosperity, harmony, and well-being? Is choosing with your Strategy rather than your head so bad when you know that using your head has been wrong before? (Caveat: Manifestors *can* make decisions from their "mind"—only eight percent of the population. And half of those still have to wait out their emotional wave. So it's really more like four percent. More about that later!)

And what happens when we're *not* following our Strategy? We might run into resistance of all sorts—whether it's a bad business deal, the wrong timing, or meeting the wrong people—if we're looking for love or a business deal. That's our choice, too, but how many trials, tribulations, wrong turns, and bad relationships do we need in order to learn our life's lessons? That's up to you.

So you have a choice in Human Design: to live up to your full potential using your Human Design Strategy, or not. Some people think of that as putting limits on what's possible. I prefer to think of it as being in alignment with what you really want. To me, that's having real abundance in life.

We have the choice in Human Design to be stressed when we're out of alignment or blissed out when we're in alignment with our Strategy. Which would you prefer? The blissful feeling comes with making decisions that are in alignment with your Strategy—you know, when you're in the flow and life is good. Those decisions just naturally *feel* better. They're the best for you, and they're right for all aspects of your current reality.

As human beings, we can consciously evolve or not. It's always our choice.

When we choose to evolve **and** use our Strategy, we're accepting the concept of Human Design, helping us stay fully alive. As part of our free will, we have the choice of living conditioned, compromised, or the more fully-alive life. A conditioned life means living your childhood conditioning. While it's hard to ever fully get *over* the conditioning we experienced as children, it's worth a try. The more you can get away from that conditioning, the more freedom you'll feel. The compromised life is one with a lot of "shoulds." You may have moved away from the conditioning of childhood, but you could still be stuck living everyone else's idea of what you *should* be doing with your life.

With the fully-alive life, you're in the driver's seat: you know your decision-making Strategy; you use it to make all your decisions; and as a result, you feel alive, aware, and engaged most of each day. This kind of freedom allows for the growth and joy that we're supposed to be here for—living out our life's purpose in a way that's congruent with our design and that just feels right and juicy!

Steve Jobs is an example of moving beyond conditioning, for the most part remaining uncompromised and living fully alive. The movie about him came out a few years ago, but I found a video recently from an early interview. This excerpt is part of a longer interview. It's a short and sweet quote. There's not all that much complexity to living fully alive—at least he sets it up as a simple concept. Here's the world as Steve Jobs saw it:

> *"When you grow up, you tend to get told the world is the way it is and your job is just to live your life inside the world. Try not to bash into the walls too much. Try to have a nice family, have fun, save a little money.*
>
> *That's a very limited life. Life can be much broader once you discover one simple fact: Everything around you that you call life was made up by people that were no smarter than you, and you can change it, you can influence it, you can build your own things that other people can use.*
>
> *Once you learn that, you'll never be the same again."*

I love having choices, don't you?

The Law of Attraction

We get what we focus on, and therefore, our thoughts create the things in our life. That's basically what the Law of Attraction says. Different teachers say it in different ways, but that's the gist of it.

Full disclosure: Not everyone believes it's a "law," but I do. I've seen it in action too many times not to. There are also a lot of people who misuse or misunderstand it. And there are loads of people who make money on courses trying to assure you of riches via the Law of Attraction. In my humble opinion, those courses won't work because that's not what the Law of Attraction is really about.

It is about getting you what you want, and that's not usually money, even if you think it is. Sorry!

If you're focusing on the past—regrets, suffering, transgressions, that bad meal you had, or even a bad cold—whether you did it or someone did it to you,that's what you'll get more of. Our attention to something is what allows more of that in. And it becomes a self-fulfilling prophecy.

Those who worry about getting a cold or the flu usually have something to worry about. If you focus on health, whether it's good health or bad health, that's what you get more of. Same thing in other areas of your life: relationships, parenting, career, etc.
As Henry Ford said, "Whether you think you can or think you can't, you're right."

In my experience and with my clients, I've put the Human Design Strategy together with the Law of Attraction to achieve the goals that we're looking for. I have found that there is an extra piece of this puzzle—as there is with most ideologies. *If* you can create a list of your intentions—detailed descriptions of what you want, be clear about it, and then trust that it will happen—you will be guided to take actions that will lead you there, according to your Human Design Strategy. I'll be honest, the last piece—the trust in the Universe/God/Higher Being—is the toughest to really understand and internalize. But it can happen. And that's what brings lasting change for you and your family.

When trust becomes a habit, everything changes—like when you don't think about shifting the car when you know how, or how to brush your teeth. Make it a habit. (We'll talk about trust and creating real clarity around your goals more in later chapters.)

So now that we've talked about following your Strategy and the Law of Attraction a bit, how can we put these together to find the real you—the authentic you—so you can be the authentic you in all your relationships? Do you need to change your story a bit to get to be the authentic you? And what about the fears that hold us back sometimes? These are the other pieces of the Human Design puzzle.

Are You Being The Authentic YOU?

It could be a simple "yes" or "no" answer, but for many of us, the reality is usually "Huh? What does that even mean?" We sometimes don't know what that means for ourselves. But, ironically, we know *very* well what it means for other people. We have this radar that senses quite accurately when someone is being authentic or not. We see this at gatherings, especially the holiday parties or networking events, when someone is acting out, showing off, or hiding out miserably in the corner. Those aren't their authentic selves, and we know it. But we put up with it, or laugh along, or ignore them, knowing it will be over soon enough. We like to be with people who are being authentic, who like themselves, and who let us into their world with a little vulnerability—whether it's a wise understanding, a short story of imperfection, or a knowing nod.

We can tell quite easily when someone is being authentic. Again, it's like radar. We know when a person is telling a story that rings true because they're feeling confident, even a little bold; they're seemingly happy, and they may even be glowing a little. That's a story that we're likely to listen to, enjoying the experience and even resonating with it a bit. It seems like more and more people are telling their "stories"—some with great success and others with more mixed reviews. I've been thinking about this lately because of some of the news that's come out about certain celebrities and figures in the news. Their story rings true when they ring true, too. If they're fearful, lashing out, or complaining bitterly about all the things that life has thrown at them, we tend to recoil. It's just a natural reaction. No one likes to hear dirty laundry aired just for the sake of media attention while claiming victimhood. It's downright cringe-worthy!

On the other hand, when the storyteller is telling the story as if it's their "hero's journey," that's a story worth listening to. That storyteller is one who has lived through the crises, taken responsibility for their actions, and then figured out a way to tell a story that doesn't scare people, but empowers, educates, and makes a distinction for them that's new and different. That's a good story! We can all learn from those stories, and we really have a thirst for those. Just look at some of the numbers on social media. The best YouTube videos of the year happened to include not one campaign ad! There is mostly uplifting, empowering, and generally positive stuff amongst the "reality" of nasty politics, divisive issues about the police, racism, gender equality, the #MeToo and #TimesUp movements, and lots of war-torn areas around the world! What a year it's been!

And yet, the background to a whirlwind year for the planet is: What happened for you? How did you progress—or not—over the past year? Were you able to get closer to the real you? Did you make yourself a priority even a little bit? Were you able to do more of the things that make you happy—and less of the things that don't? And if we're so good at seeing other people's authenticity, why can't we see or manage or improve our own authenticity more easily?

Back to the authentic you and me. What is it that makes the story authentic when we're not exactly sure who we are? So, if we break that up a little, we've got being authentic vs. knowing who we are. We can solve the second part first with a humble but blatant plug for Human Design. That can help you to figure out who you really are by delving into the details of what makes you tick. What makes you the unique you that you are and the parts of you that will never change. Hopefully, that's why you're reading this so far.

Once you know who you are, the rest of the journey to authenticity is easy or at least easier. When we know who we are, it feels good because that's who we're supposed to be. It's not forced; it's just a natural way of being. That's part of the reason that the ones we like the best tell their story most comfortably. We even call it "comfortable in their own skin" when an actor or author matures into their roles. They figure out who they are, why they're doing what they're doing, and then do it with grace and ease, wisdom and confidence. The confidence comes in part from performing their role—whatever industry they're in—with competence. Once you're competent at something, you gain confidence. And the competence/confidence cycle continues on to make you a "natural." But that "natural" title that we give people who seem to be happy in the work they do is a bit of a misnomer, or at least an overstatement. They are happy because they love what they're doing. They didn't choose something that they *hated* and made themselves fall in love with it. They naturally gravitated toward, and made a choice, doing something that they already loved, or at least liked doing. And then the doing became a joy for them. It's one of the reasons that I'm such a fan of getting kids exposed to as many things as possible before they reach high school. Many of us don't find what we love until our second career, and some are serial career lovers with many careers in tow! Whatever feels right for you, whatever makes you happy is the real you asserting itself! Yes, it's a cliché by now, but do what you love and the rest will follow. If you are the one celebrating your own energy—fully, without holding back, and being the you that you were born to be—no one will look away, and it will be a great story because you're being the authentic you!

So What is This Thing we Call Fear??

Some fears will never go away completely—like a fear of snakes, perhaps—but I don't usually "do" fear. I used to think of myself as "fearless" or at least as a survivor. I've had my share of fear over the years, of course, but I actually avoid talking about it, unless it serves a client. So, as I've been thinking about it lately, I realized that maybe I'm not giving fear its due. Maybe I've been avoiding it and doing my clients a disservice. Maybe it *is* time to talk about fear a bit more. And maybe this book was just the impetus I needed to respond to!

Let's do a little review of what Human Design is as a set-up for the next part, where we'll delve into some of the fears in the chart and how they might affect you.

Further Clarity: What is Human Design??

To me, Human Design is where science and spirituality come together. It's a very practical system for human beings—an instruction manual for your life really. It's a personality assessment tool that's only been around since 1987. It's a combination of a number of ancient wisdoms—the Kabbalah, the I'Ching, the Hindu Chakra system, and astrology, in terms of where the planets were aligned when you were born, as well as quantum physics, bio-genetics, and modern math, on the modern side. Put those all together and the synergistic result is called Human Design.

As you look at a chart, it's like looking at your DNA; it's what makes you unique and as individual as a snowflake. There's no one like you, so wouldn't it be nice to know who that is and what you're really here for? What would make you happy, joyful, fulfilled, and continually growing? I think of joy, fulfillment, and growth as a cycle in life. And it's probably fair to say that whether you're looking for that or you've already got some of it, you want more of it.

The thing is: We all want *more*—more clarity, more self-awareness, more spirituality, and yes, more stuff, too—and less fear, less distractions, less worries. You're probably also looking for meaning in your life—and asking the questions like "Why am I here? Who am I, and what should I be doing with my life?" But also, **how can I make more money at something that's fulfilling**? So Human Design is a very cool tool to help you get there.

The chart shows you your energetic blueprint, your decision-making Strategy, and your life's purpose, plus a whole lot more. It's very specific and very accurate information about what makes you you—what makes you unique on the planet.

It's about personality traits, your strengths and weaknesses. And by the way, what we consider to be weaknesses are actually our life lessons—what we're here to learn from. The chart you got is the perfection of you when you were born. A lot of times we forget how perfect we were when we were born. Human Design readings help you to remember that perfection *and* allow you to see how you can move closer to being the you that you're here to be.

Not as a perfect human being, but as the you you were meant to be. Before we got conditioned by our very well-meaning parents and teachers, or siblings and friends. Before everyone had suggestions for who we *should* grow up to be, rather than allowing us to find out for ourselves. And as much as they want good stuff for us, they don't really know what's on our chart, the life plan that we came in with.

It's beautiful, and it's powerful, and we can see it on the chart when we do a Human Design session. I'm actually looking forward to the day when parents *do* get their child's Human Design chart on the day they're born. Wouldn't that change the world for the better? Wouldn't you want that for your children or grandchildren?

OK, sorry for the rant. With that clarity around some of the principles of Human Design, now let's move on to talking about fears and where they show up in the chart.

What Does Each Energy Type Fear?

Each Energy Type has its own fears because we wonder what will happen if we *don't* follow our Strategy to get what we want. Even if you didn't always consciously know your Human Design Strategy, you **may** have figured it out, or you may have had a sense of what it is. But whether we know our Strategy or not, we always know when it's *not* working, don't we? When we don't get what we want, when we don't get the job, or the date, or the new car? When we keep running into resistance, things just aren't going our way and nothing seems to be working out for us? Life is throwing us a curveball, we say, and we have no idea that it's just because we're *not* following our Strategy. But each Energy Type is different...

So for the Manifestor, they're afraid that they're being too powerful or that they're forced to hide their power because of cultural reasons or gender reasons. They also worry that their anger keeps them from fulfilling their power. That kind of forceful energy getting jammed down usually affects their health and overall well-being. It's like putting a Mentos in Coke and shaking it up. Boom!

For Generators and Manifesting Generators, they fear that they'll never have something to respond to. They worry that they're impatiently settling for less, not getting what they want, or don't have the patience to wait out their mastery of a career. They also worry that their frustration is keeping them from achieving mastery—when they hop from one job, or even career, to another whenever they get frustrated, instead of waiting it out.

For Projectors, because of their Strategy of waiting for the invitation, they constantly worry and really fear that the invitation will never come, that their waiting will be in vain. They worry that they're not good enough—and yet, if *they* don't value themselves, no one else will either. Also, their default emotion is bitterness, so if others feel the bitterness from a Projector, it keeps them away and masks the value of the Projector.

And finally, for Reflectors, they worry that if they're always taking on other people's energy, how will they know if they're being themselves or if they're somehow merging with other energies. That's a tough call, because they really have to be away from other people to understand their own energy. They have to really tease out what *is* their energy vs. what they're reflecting. They have such potential for the wisdom of humanity, and so they need to be with people. That's a real conundrum for Reflectors.

If you know your Energy Type, you probably identified with one of the fears above. There are also other fears in the chart having to do with nervousness, anxiety, and survival—that are associated with the Solar Plexus, Ajna, and Spleen—but the ones above are associated with the Energy Types.

And as you probably realize, none of us are free from fears. It's all part of being human. When we look at our Human Design, we can see the fears that are unique to us and at the very least give each one a name. Knowing this will give you tremendous insight into your personality and how you operate.

There are lots of things we can be afraid of in our lives, but decision-making does **not** need to be one of them. You *can* let go of that fear whenever you choose to start living according to your Strategy.

As Ra says, it will be a deep relief that there's nothing wrong with you. Fear is to be recognized and understood. Once you are aware of the fears in your chart, and then understand them over time, you'll find ways to step through them so that they're not the problems or blocks that they once were. And then they can be appreciated for what they are: ways to keep us safe in new situations. Isn't that a good thing?

Goals

Goals in Relationships

It's probably safe to assume that most of us want to have harmonious relationships. Life is so much better when everyone is getting along, isn't it? But how often does that happen? Is your home generally fun, active, goal-oriented, with goals and intentions set up each year as individuals, as a couple, and as a family? Or are you living week to week with schedules, priorities, and ever-changing goals?

Of course, we'd all like to get along, but it's so elusive. Think of it like this: We can have two Human Design charts that are very similar. Let's say they were born just a few months apart—as many high school or college classmates would be—and actually have the same Energy Centers defined (different gates, but the same centers). Guess what? They'll have a lot of the same gates, a lot of the same values, likes and dislikes. But after a while (maybe after a few years of dating or marriage), things get boring. There's very little for them to explore together, and there's nowhere to vent when needed. It just doesn't work.

It's like playing chopsticks on the piano. Do you remember those notes, or have you heard it? Two fingers playing exactly the same notes in different keys. That's what it's like to have two people with similar charts.

So that's not really the ideal, would you agree?

Much better to have a complex classical music or jazz tune on the piano, where all kinds of things are happening and all things are possible. It sounds exciting, alive, vibrant. That's when relationships flourish!

And that's why people with variations in their charts will be attracted to each other. Like most other places in life, opposites attract. People with the emotional Solar Plexus undefined will be attracted to people who have it defined. They're attracted to each other exactly because one is more emotional than the other. Same with the Will Center. Someone who doesn't have willpower will be attracted to someone who seems to have the willpower to get all kinds of things done.

Here's the thing about relationships: The more people there are (three or more) in a family, the more likely it is that two or more of your Human Design charts will have places that are electro-magnetics (two gates coming together to form a channel or road between two energy centers), and these usually feel good. But there are also just as likely to be places in the chart that can cause conflict. These are not horrible by any means. They're just places in the chart where you'll want to be aware of what's going on so that you can deal with it.

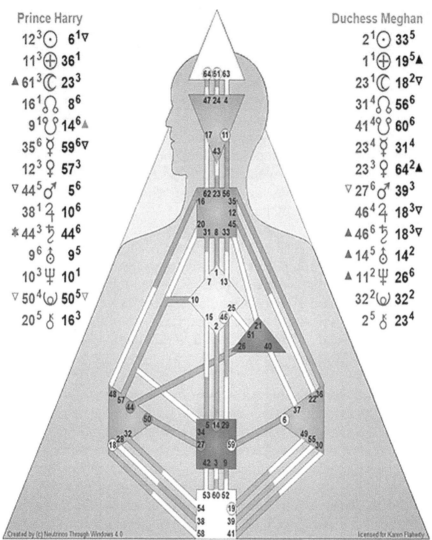

**Composite Human Design chart for
Prince Harry and Duchess Meghan**

For example, one parent may have the Gate 15 defined in their chart, while the other parent may have the Gate 5 defined. Together, these make up one completed channel and form an electro-magnetic. These are usually good in a relationship. However, with this channel, the Gate 5 is all about Rhythms and patterns in life, and the

Gate 15 is all about Extremes. With the Gate 5, that parent will be the one to get all the kids up each morning with ease, eating, exercising, and sleeping on a fairly consistent schedule for themselves, and helping the rest of the household to stay in sync. It actually helps things run fairly smoothly when there's a Gate 5 in the house, even if it's one of the children. The Gate 15, on the other hand, doesn't usually run on a schedule. They are more in the flow of whatever is happening around them. While that works to finish up a project for work or school late at night and then get on a plane to present it the next day without missing a beat, the tendency to do things in the flow versus on a particular schedule can be disruptive at times for the others in the family.

Can you see how one simple trait regarding schedules can become a point of contention in a home? To the person with either the Gate 5 or the Gate 15, that's normal for them. When they're in their own world, it's all good. But combine their tendencies—or preferred way of doing things—with the rest of the family, and the potential for conflict will arise. Compromise is a good solution, but it doesn't answer the *why* of it.

With Human Design, you can answer the *why* and solve some of the mystery surrounding it. Yes, Janie does have the Gate 5 and wants to have the same breakfast at the same time every morning. While her brother Matt comes down for breakfast at various times—or not at all because he's been up all night working on a paper—and asks why is there only oatmeal to eat, can't we change it up a bit? Both are normal behaviors for kids, but when you know *why* they are so different, it's easier to understand, to accommodate, and to ultimately allow their behavior because it's not hurting anyone. That's just the way they operate. It's how they're wired.

This example of the Gates 5 and 15 are just one of many that help to explain the various people in your life—at home and at work. Why do they act like that, you wonder?

Once you know more about yourself, it's a lot easier to understand how everyone around you works. Now let's talk about some of the other challenges and how they can be understood and eventually get to a satisfying solution.

Solutions

Now that we've discussed some of the basics challenges of human relationships, here are the two basic steps to resolving conflicts in your home, at work, and with family and friends. The first step is to understand yourself and make decisions with your own decision-making Strategy, according to your Energy Type. That alone will change the way things appear to unfold at home and at work. The next step, once you're making decisions that you're happier with, is to allow those around you to make their own decisions. This might be your spouse, children, boss, colleagues, parents, etc. "Allowing" will look different in various situations, of course, but your allowance will look and feel like acceptance, a lack of judgment, and generally appreciation and love of that person.

And that's it. Very simple. Not so easy.

Start practicing with those two steps first. Then when you're feeling more comfortable with your own decisions and observing others as they make their decisions, there are some other things to take into consideration. What I'll get into below are other ways to help make a relationship work more smoothly. These are the places where I find clients say it's a challenge to "allow" this or that activity. Here we're describing the distinctions between people who have a Sacral (all the Generators) and those who don't—and what that feels like in relationships. Next, we look at the Throat Center and how that plays into relationships of all kinds. Finally, we look at the Solar Plexus, which is the center for our emotions. With these distinctions, we tread onto the field where other people's decisions can feel like an affront to us. Situations where you may feel like that's not fair, not acceptable, and "who do they think they are?" territory.

Generators Versus the Other Energy Types

Why do some kids or colleagues have energy *all* the time and others just don't? I'm sure this has occurred to you at work and at school, and perhaps even at home. Generators and Manifesting Generators *do* have a big Motor in their bodies called the Sacral. It's what makes them Generators. They can just go and go, every day and on the weekends, too. As kids, they can barely sit still in class and play outside as long as they can. As teens, they go out for three teams and have a job after school. As adults, they have a job or two, a few kids, and lots of community activities to keep them busy. They make up about seventy percent of the population—that's a lot of Generators! And so their default belief is that everyone has that kind of energy.

And that would be incorrect. In Human Design, the other thirty percent of the population are made up of Projectors, Manifestors, and Reflectors. They *don't* have that Sacral defined, and so they don't have that Energizer Bunny energy like the Generators. They do *try* to keep up with the Generators. And in a way, they can fake that Generator energy, because when they're around Generators, they are always taking in the Sacral energy and then amplifying it. So in school or at work, the non-Sacral types *seem* to be keeping up, and they might even think they are running circles around their classmates—for a while. When they get home, they are tired. They need a nap or are early to bed, and usually need more sleep than the Generator children—and that happens all through their lives.

And there's nothing wrong with this. They're not lazy—they just don't have that Sacral energy that so much of the world has. While they may *say* they want to go out for a few teams like their friends, if you asked them what they *really* want, they would tell you that they really only want to concentrate on one team each year. And that would be much better for them physically and emotionally. Same thing at work. Careers that are more flexible—like teaching and sales, or where they can make their own hours as an entrepreneur—are much more suitable for them.

Can you see the conflicts or misunderstandings that might occur in a family or work environment?

- Why does one child get to nap while the others are doing chores?

- Why is one child the star of the football team and the other is quite satisfied with Chess Club?

- Why does one colleague get to leave early while the others stay late?

- Why is one child always sick while the others are usually healthy?

- At a conference, why can some colleagues attend all sessions *and* party all night, while others are turning in early?

Most of these situations are the kinds that come across to Generator types as unfair, but once we understand that the non-Sacral types need a different schedule or a little more time to complete a project or just more down time, it's usually workable.

Ironically, it's usually the Projectors who feel like life isn't fair. After all, they're not shirking their responsibilities, but they do wonder why they just don't seem to have the energy that most other people do. In another twist of fate, once the Projectors get their projects completed, they are often superior to the others because of the wisdom that goes into their execution of any task. The awareness of this non-Sacral design can be a huge leg up in helping to understand these energy dynamics.

Having a Voice in the Matter

Of the five Energy Types, only two have a voice that can be heard easily: the Manifestors and the Manifesting Generators. That's about forty percent of the population. The rest have a much harder time being heard as Generators, Projectors, and Reflectors. The

Manifestors and Manifesting Generators will always have a motorized Throat—that means it's connected to a Motor, and makes it very easy to be heard above most other people. They also have an energy about them that people recognize as someone who can get things done with that voice—whether it's making introductions, referrals, match-making, or just having a good time and telling a good story. As a result, they make wonderful sales people, leaders of all sorts, managers, trainers, and entrepreneurs.

The other sixty percent of the population *do not* have a motorized Throat. Their Throat on their chart might be defined or open. Either way, it's not connected to a motor that would give them a voice that's heard easily. They may *think* that they can be heard, and they can be heard with people they know—family, friends, co-workers. But not with strangers, not when others aren't expecting them to say something and not when others are talking.

For example, you may think that your voice carries and you're usually heard, especially if you're in a managerial position. But what happens when a number of people are all talking in a meeting and you're trying to get their attention? Or if you're trying to talk over someone else? Or if you and someone else talk at the same moment? Are you the one who's heard, or is it the person with the motorized Throat, who's used to talking and being heard all the time—and also usually takes it for granted?

What happens in a family situation? The person with the loudest voice usually wins, right? I'm the oldest of six, and as a Generator with an open Throat, they only heard me when I raised my voice to try to be heard. And the irony is that when a non-motorized Throat tries to talk louder, it sounds like we're yelling or upset. It just doesn't sound right, and people tend to cringe.

Early on, I learned to ask my younger brother, the Manifestor, to get everyone's attention before I tried to say something. (I didn't know about Human Design yet, but when John said, "Hey," everyone listened!) And it worked! Later on, I felt I needed a voice that could be heard in my corporate positions. I took many classes on voice:

singing lessons with a Broadway voice teacher, assertiveness training, a week-long public speaking course. All in the hopes of having a voice that would be heard in any situation, but to no avail. While I was projecting my voice better in meetings, the clerk at CVS still didn't hear me as I tried to say hello or get their attention, unless they were looking at my moving lips. This can be very frustrating!

Once you know about Human Design and your own Throat's definition, it's much easier to see where and when others can be heard or not. As a Manifestor or Manifesting Generator, I tell my clients they should take the lead in making introductions, referrals, and helping others be heard at a networking event or meeting. The rest of the population really appreciates any help they can get!

And this generosity applies at home, too. If there's one or more child without the motorized Throat, that child should always be given an opportunity to speak. Many times, especially as children, the motorized Throat will dominate the conversation. They're usually funny and witty and full of stories, so most parents and siblings don't mind it. But it's much better for everyone's self-esteem to give each child a chance to practice making points and generally having a family discussion rather than just one person talking—parent or child.

Who do You Think is Emotional??

The Emotional Solar Plexus (the triangle on the right side of the body graph) is the one Energy Center that can be perplexing to explain and sometimes perplexing to understand and take in. Half the world has the Solar Plexus defined, and half the world has it open. We all have our own set of emotions, of course. That's no surprise. The difference between the two lies in the expression of those emotions. The people who are defined have a **wave** of emotions that goes up and down on a regular basis. The other half—who are open at the Solar Plexus—*do not* have a wave. They tend to be more even-keeled in their emotions—sometimes a little high, sometimes a little low, but not on a schedule as those with the wave are.

With the emotional wave and the Solar Plexus defined, these are people who can usually feel their wave of emotions changing from time to time. Some people's waves can be quite short, changing in a day or two; some much longer—up to two years. Some are relatively mild; others can be very wild mood swings. The waves definitely vary from person to person, but each person can keep track of their wave on a calendar in order to determine its length, which is good to know and easy to track as High or Low day to day. Also notice that your emotions don't change if other people are around. If you're in a great mood, that's what your friends and family will see. But your emotions are what they are, and if you're down, no cajoling or kind words will help—until the mood changes.

With no emotional wave and the Solar Plexus open, the other half of the population do indeed have their own set of emotions on any given day. But when you are with other people, some of those people will be emotionally defined. And you *will* take in those emotions and amplify them. And all of a sudden, you have the feeling of different emotions than what you walked into the room with. If that emotional person is feeling happy, like at a wedding, then you'll take in those emotions, amplify them, and you'll feel as happy or even more so. On the other hand, if the emotional person is sad or angry or depressed or in grief, as at a funeral, you will take in those emotions also. And then you'll feel that way, too. I'm usually the first one crying at a funeral because my Solar Plexus is open.

The solution for the open Solar Plexus is to act like a screen and not a sponge. Take in the emotions that you feel, but like a window screen, let them pass through you. You don't need to hold on to them. Those emotions usually don't serve you, and so, once you recognize them, it's best to get rid of them as soon as possible.

Here are just a few of the kinds of situations the Solar Plexus (SP) can cause:

- Open SP people tend to be people-pleasers in order to avoid conflict.

- Defined SP people tend to run the energy of the office or the home. If they're in a good mood, everyone is; if not, no one's happy.

- Between an open and defined SP, the conflicts can escalate because the energies are literally bouncing back and forth between the two. The best idea is to take a break, leave the room, and reconvene later.

- An open SP person might innocently ask a defined SP person, "What's wrong?" and get an earful or just a dirty look. The open SP has just energetically picked up on the bad mood of the defined SP, while the defined SP is trying to hide their bad mood. Unfortunately, there's not much hiding when it comes to energy.

The real irony I find with clients is that a lot of times the person who is defined emotionally will think that they are very good at hiding their emotions from others, and therefore, describe themselves as unemotional. Over time, of course, they do tend to operate on a relatively even keel with few, if any, outbursts. But even if they are "hiding" their external expressions of emotions, the energetic wave is still there, and others will feel it.

And on the other hand, the people who are open emotionally think that *they* are the ones who are emotional. Many clients will actually fight me on this because they've lived for forty years or more thinking that *they* were the emotional one in their family. (And I don't blame them. This was my experience, too, when I first heard about my Human Design.) Meanwhile this is their conditioning from their birth family. They took in all those emotions for so long that they don't know what it's like to have *only* their emotions as a basis. Once they realize that if they were to go off by themselves for a few days, they would most certainly be even-keeled emotionally; they are able to relax into the realization that their emotions are just fine the way they are—cool, calm, and collected. Ahhh!

The Family Who Understands Each Other

There are many examples from my clients of families who got along much better after they realized their Human Design charts and Strategies. But I thought I'd use these two new parents as an example of getting along when the Energy Types, Strategies and emotions are all completely different:

Celebrity Profile in Relationship: George Clooney & Amal Alamuddin

George: Emotional Projector born on May 6, 1961, at 2:58 am in Lexington, KY
Amal: Manifesting Generator (non-emotional) born on February 3, 1978, in Beirut, Lebanon

On September 12, 2014, an actor/activist married a lawyer/activist. It was a quiet family gathering joining two people in love in Milan. And it would have gone largely unnoticed by many, except that one of the people was George Clooney!

In one fell swoop, one of the world's most eligible bachelors was single no more! But what made this rather self-confirmed bachelor take notice of Amal Alamuddin *and* propose when so many other long-term girlfriends were told there would be no chance of a proposal—ever?

I've always been a fan of his, but on this change of behavior, many people were surprised, so it always helps to take a look at their Human Design charts. And since Amal is now in the news quite a bit, I was able to find her birth date. (No birth time yet, but I chose 8pm as the most likely timing, given the moon gates and the profile it provided.)

Since we can probably assume that most people know who George Clooney is and no one really knew much about Amal as they married, let's look at the charts for each of them and then take a look at their charts together.

George is an emotional Projector with just two centers and one channel defined in his chart. This makes him a very "open" Projector; that is, one who takes in a lot of energy from other people. When he was younger, he took in other people's energy at work or at play and just kept going and going. But as he got older, it likely crept up on him and affected his health. Now that he's turned fifty, he can be more discerning in his acting roles, his travels, and in his choice of companions.

With just a Will Center and Emotional Solar Plexus defined, he thought he could keep up with everyone else and could will himself to keep going or finish a project or keep a promise to someone. But again, his choices are likely becoming more wise in ways that help him to moderate his activities so that his health and his stamina are priorities for him. He is emotional, but the wave is likely a mild one. The only channel that's defined is the Channel of Agreements between the Will and the Solar Plexus. This makes him someone who will never break a promise. And if he does, he'll feel ill about it. This may help to explain why after one marriage and divorce when he was younger, he would rather tell women up front in a relationship that he would not be marrying them than to give them or anyone else the impression that he was "stringing them along."

Amal is a non-emotional Manifesting Generator. She has had a fast-track career as a lawyer, author, and as an activist, has been quite involved in humanitarian activities—which is how she caught George's eye in the first place. She speaks three languages, has studied at Oxford and NYU, and specializes in international law, criminal law, and human rights. She's bright, beautiful, and has been very successful in her career, including representing some very polarizing clients.

As a Manifesting Generator, she has had the Sacral energy as well as the Will to accomplish whatever she sets out to do. She, like George, will never break a promise. Her defined channels are the Channel of the Alpha ('nuf said), the Channel of Transmission (also known as the Channel of the Salesperson), and the Channel of Resources (making money and knowing how to use it wisely). Putting those themes together, you can see how as a Manifesting Generator with both the energy and the voice to make things happen, as well as the themes of money, power, and sales, she's made a name for herself in a relatively short time as a barrister. She's even written a book and articles that have gained her notoriety as a speaker to young adults.

Her profile is the Hermit/Opportunist, and while naturally quiet, she also has a knack for stepping into the opportunities that are correct for her. It makes her a "natural" at almost anything she decides to try.

Now, as we put George and Amal's charts together, we get a very interesting picture. Usually, we look for how many gates match up from one chart to the other. Here there is only *one* electro-magnetic match-up: the Channel 5-15. One electro-magnetic is good, but more are better for most relationships.

However, what we find is that George and Amal *share* the same Incarnation Cross—the Right Angle Cross of the Sphinx. The Incarnation Cross is the mythology of your life *if* you are following your Strategy. So while George was born in May, and Amal was born in February, the Crosses repeat in each quarter, and so their Crosses happen to be the same. This means that the four gates in their Sun and Earth are exactly the same (just in a different order), so they have the same four gates that make up about seventy percent of their personality traits. George's Cross focuses on Resources (as the Gate 2 is in his Conscious Sun), while Amal is the Listener, as the Gate 13 is in her Conscious Sun. It really fits so well with both her career and relationships; people will just love confiding in her and knowing that their secrets are safe. What an apt fit for someone like George, who is always in the public eye and would feel the need for a safe haven in his confidante and wife.

In a way, they've found their twin flame. No wonder they're so compatible, and not surprisingly, the relationship progressed to engagement quickly. More than a heightened electric charge between them, there is a calm in knowing the other person so intimately with understanding. In addition to the four gates in the Incarnation Cross, they have a few other gates in common, which makes for additional shared values. They have a wide range of gates in common: Gate 21–Control; Gate 44–Alertness; Gate 56–The Storyteller; Gate 60–Evolution; and Gate 17–Opinions. Gates 21 and 17 can be the "troublemakers" in a relationship, but since they both have them, it gets canceled out, to an extent!

With so many shared values and common humanitarian interests, this seems like a wonderful relationship for both of them! And, of course, the addition of the little ones in 2017 only adds to the family dynamics, as the twins, Ella and Alexander, are both Generators. With three Sacrals in the house now, George will be outnumbered!

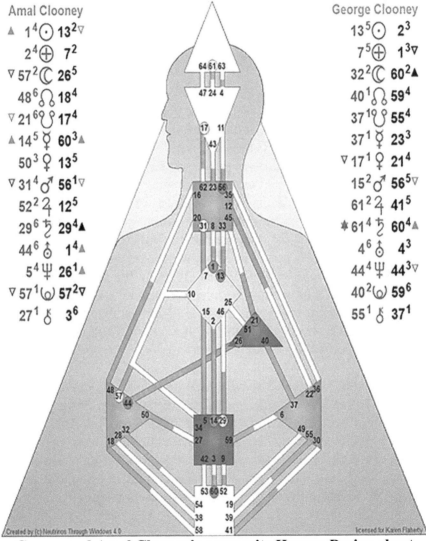

George and Amal Clooney's composite Human Design chart

Relationships make the world go round, and they can sometimes stop us from growing and fulfilling our wishes, hopes, and dreams. You deserve to have all those fulfilled. I hope that you're seeing a way in, out, or around your current relationships so that you can get what you want and so can they! These are not huge pronouncements; they're just little distinctions that allow you to look at things in a new way. Kind of like how the Inuits have multiple words for snow. It's like that.

Now let's take a look at how these kinds of distinctions can affect your health and well-being.

Chapter 3
Your Health

Most Common Health Challenges

"We are always comparing ourselves to the other. It's not about wanting to be richer, faster, smarter, all of that stuff. It's a joke. It's about recognizing that to be ourselves is the only way in which we're going to be fulfilled spiritually. In which we are going to have healthy lives, and I mean physically healthy lives. See, knowing yourself is not about a spiritual experience. It can be, but it's not what it's about. It's about being healthy human beings. It's about being healthy psychically. It's about being healthy physically. It's about being in the right vehicle that you know how to care for. It's about seeing that a healthy life is the only thing that matters. And that healthy life is about many things, but it begins with your decision-making process. And it begins with a basic understanding that Human Design brings: who you are, where you are and with whom. And everything about quality of life and everything about the beauty of your own life that can only manifest when you enter into things correctly as yourself, only then can you have the relationships that are of value to you, can you have the careers and associations that are of value to you, and can you lift the burden from yourself that you think there is something wrong. Because there isn't, and there never has been." Ra Uru Hu, 1999.

When it comes to health, there's really not much to say about the bottom line of being well in Human Design. And there's not a lot of gray in between.

Either you're following your path for your life's purpose or you're not. And as a direct result, therefore, either you're feeling well or you're not.

Happy and fulfilled and content and doing what you love = great health.

Unhappy and unfulfilled, depressed, distressed, and not doing something you love (either as a job or hobby) = poor health or illness. (And fortunately, if you're young and you're still looking for your purpose, you've got time to change before it catches up with you.)

Don't shoot the messenger. It sounds very basic, I know. And pretty simplistic. But it's true, based on my journey and many of the clients I work with.

"Dis-ease" is the lack of ease and a lack of well-being. In Human Design, the only reason that you're not feeling well is if you're not following your Strategy, living a life that pleases you, and doing what you really want to do. Your disease could be minor or serious, a bad cold or a chronic illness. Many of us have stress-induced illnesses that come from jobs we hate, pushing to make things happen that we don't really want, bosses who don't treat us well, environments that are allergens, or spouses who are not right for us. We suffer from thyroid conditions, adrenal fatigue, general burnout, autoimmune diseases, exhaustion, anxiety attacks, and more. It's not fun, no matter when it happens.

Bottom line: There is no cure for a self-induced illness except change.

The change can be gradual, or it can be quick. You can take your time researching many professions, classes, or internships. It can take months, or it can take years. Or it can be a very quick decision. For some, especially Generators and Projectors, the path can be a long and winding one. It can take a few careers over decades. For many of us, we got into the career that our parents had themselves or suggested for us. We might have spent years honing that craft or profession, only to find out that it really doesn't suit us. Then on to the next one. And perhaps the next one.

Until finally, usually around forty or fifty years old for Generators, and sometimes after retirement (and even younger for Projectors), we've found what really makes us feel contented, fulfilled, and happy to get up in the morning.

A hobby or new career that makes our hearts sing. One that we don't mind doing. Some that we don't even get paid for. Then things start to click into place, to flow for us, to make us happy to be where we are and doing what we're doing. And guess what? At that point, your health starts to improve. Because your physical body loves to be content.

If you're in a place or career where you're not feeling well, you can begin the journey to wellness now with a few small changes. The first is to begin following your Strategy.
In Human Design, one of the biggest differentiating factors from other personality tools is that it tells you how to make decisions. We call that your specific decision-making Strategy. It works for you— and it works all the time—every day for decisions large and small. It seems simple, doesn't it?

When I talk with clients, however, it gets a bit more complicated. It's not because the Strategy doesn't work. It works! But we can be swayed in our decisions sometimes by other factors, like other people's energy!
Here's a quick review of the decision-making Strategies for each Energy Type:

- Manifestors: Inform others (who need to know) before you act.

- Generators: Wait to respond with your gut.

- Manifesting Generators: Wait to respond with your gut, then let others know (inform) before you take action.

- Projectors: Wait for the invitation on the big decisions in life (and wait to be asked for advice)

- Reflectors: Wait for 28 days when making a big decision.

Beyond the Strategies for each Energy Type, there is also an Authority that flavors each Strategy, no matter which Energy Type you are. There are seven Authorities, and they are determined by which Energy Centers you have defined. They work in conjunction with the Strategy for your type. Think of it as a kind of second opinion on the decisions you're making.

The most common Authority is Emotional Authority, which has to do with the defined Solar Plexus. This is the Authority for about half the population (fifty percent!). While waiting out the emotional wave to tell you whether to make a big decision or not, you are also following the Strategy for your Energy Type. For example, a Generator type would have a gut response to some big decision, but then need to wait out the emotional wave to make sure that you like that new car on a good day or a not-so-good day. If you get all "yes" responses, then it's a good decision. If not, it may not be the right timing. Similarly for Projectors, you may get a big invitation, but you'll want to wait out the wave to make sure it's correct for you.

Many of us are just pure Sacral beings—where our Sacral is our Authority as well as our Strategy. We just have to respond to things in our outside reality—and that's it. Nothing else should really affect our decisions. Sacral Authority is probably about another third of the population.

The other five Authorities are more rare and kind of get into the weeds of details. There are videos on my website and others' that get into all the details of Authority. But you always want to pay attention to *your* Authority in addition to following your Strategy.

So if we know our Strategy and Authority, what makes it challenging to follow them all the time? What makes it more complicated?
As they try to follow their Strategy, what also comes into play for many people are the Energy Centers we have that are open (white on your chart). These open centers take in energy from others and operate in funny ways sometimes. They become the "what if" questions we ask ourselves after we think we've made a decision. Let's look at some of these and how they make decisions more difficult.

As we talk about the Energy Centers, here is a chart of all the Energy Centers (and what they do) so you can follow along with your own chart.

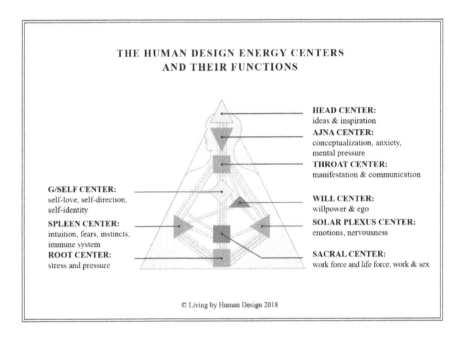

THE HUMAN DESIGN ENERGY CENTERS
AND THEIR FUNCTIONS

HEAD CENTER:
ideas & inspiration

AJNA CENTER:
conceptualization, anxiety, mental pressure

THROAT CENTER:
manifestation & communication

G/SELF CENTER:
self-love, self-direction, self-identity

SPLEEN CENTER:
intuition, fears, instincts, immune system

ROOT CENTER:
stress and pressure

WILL CENTER:
willpower & ego

SOLAR PLEXUS CENTER:
emotions, nervousness

SACRAL CENTER:
work force and life force, work & sex

© Living by Human Design 2018

Thinking about all the factors that can lead us to doubt our own Strategy for making decisions, they line up rather neatly into two categories:

Not Listening to our own Strategy	Centers in Play
Saying "YES" when we mean "NO"	Solar Plexus, Will, Sacral, Root
Saying "NO" when we mean "YES"	Spleen, Head/Ajna, Solar Plexus, G

If you're making a decision that's bigger than what to have for dinner, you may have come to rely on—and even fully trust—your own decision-making Strategy over time. But then something happens to change your mind or change your perspective. What is that?? And where does it come from?

SAYING "YES" WHEN YOU MEAN "NO"

So you've checked in with your Strategy, and let's suppose the answer you've come up with is *"no."* And you're feeling pretty sure about it. It feels right to you.
Your "No" may sound like this:

- "No, I really don't want to buy a new car right now."

- "No, I don't want to go with the entire extended family on another summer vacation."

- "No, I don't feel like I need to be at the office for a third evening this week."

- "No, I really don't have the energy to help out with this all-weekend fundraiser."

But then, against your own internal advice, you wind up saying "YES" to one of these situations. And you wonder why—how did this happen again? (And at this point you may be asking, "What does this have to do with my health?" Just wait—you'll see!)

Does any of this sound familiar? If you have an open Will, Root, Sacral or Solar Plexus, they may sound like you. And here's why: You're taking in energy from someone else that's making you question the decision you've made. Here's an example:

If your Will Center is open (white), you may have walked into the car dealership with a real desire to see what's new after doing a little research at home, but knowing that you intend to buy something in six months or a year from now. Not today. The reason doesn't matter; it's your decision. It just feels better to wait. Of course, you are asking a few questions and are assisted by an incredibly smooth-talking salesperson who assures you, after looking at a few cars, that the prices and interest rates will go up, this car won't be around for long, and blah, blah, blah. Before you know it, you've signed the paperwork for a brand-new car. What happened?

Basically, the salesperson's Will Center energy was absorbed and amplified by your own open Will Center. And that energy felt very good. In fact, it felt empowering. All of a sudden, the cautious patience to wait for six months seemed a little silly—and the amplified willpower was egging you on: "Come on, you can do this. Why wait? You love it, right?" And ironically, when this willpower is amplified, we also want to *please* whoever is doing the asking! The salesperson usually has no idea of all this energy moving around. They know they're good at their job; they just don't realize it's all about energy and not as much about what they're saying. They really don't have to say all that much! And yet, you, with the open Will Center, credit card, and signature at the ready, are "sold" on the idea of a new car.

My suggestion to clients is to completely *remove* yourself from the energy in the dealership, and particularly from that salesperson, so that you can make a decision on your own—*without* their energy to persuade you. Or you can bring someone with you—your wingman—to make sure that you don't buy anything that day.

And don't worry, if it is a really good deal, it will be there tomorrow or next week—when you've had a little time to think about it without other energies to fog your judgment one way or the other.

If you have the open Solar Plexus, you are similarly taking in other people's emotions. So you may want to say "no" in a certain situation, but because you feel the other person's emotions—either good or not-so-good—you're persuaded to change your mind and say "yes." You may feel badly for them, or compassionate for their circumstances, or even empathetic—where you feel what they're feeling. Any of these feelings—that are *not yours*—will have the effect of making you less solid about your decision.

If you have the open Sacral, you will be taking in the sustainable energy of lots of people around you. This energy makes you feel like you've got lots of energy to go and go, when you're around it. But when you go home, you feel tired. When at a large group gathering—like a party, conference, or networking event—you'll feel like you have energy and want to stay to play, party, or network. In Human Design, we describe this feeling as "not knowing when enough is enough." So it feels like the pressure to say, "Yes, I'll stay a while longer," when you really want to go home and get some rest. Knowing your own energy and its limits helps in this instance. Sometimes you may have the energy to stay out longer, but it's always best to check in with yourself first.

If you have the open Root, this one just feels like pressure from other people. Whether it's your spouse, business partner, your manager, or your children, you will feel their defined Root stress, and it will make you say things you don't really mean to say. The sheer feeling of pressure from their defined Root—they don't even have to say anything—will make you rush or move more quickly, even if there's no reason to. It makes me rush across a street when I feel like traffic is waiting for me, rush when I'm getting ready to go out with my husband, or get nervous around the boss (when I had a boss). We will do anything to get rid of that feeling of pressure, including saying "yes" when we really want to say "no."

Does any of that sound familiar?

The best way around the pressure that the open Root Center feels is self-awareness. Once you realize what that feeling of pressure is, it's a lot easier to recognize it for what it is, stop for a moment, and then ask yourself what choice to make in this situation. Do you need to rush? Do you need to ask a question for clarity? Is there really a deadline that needs to be met? Can you ask for a little more time to work on a project? Can you tell your child they can get a toy *next* time? These are all questions to figure out if the stress you're feeling is yours or if you're reacting to someone else's stress. (Note to self: you've got enough stress without taking on the stress from others.)

Those are some of the really common ways that we wind up saying "*yes*" when we really want to say "*no*." It makes us feel like we have no control, no willpower, irrational emotions, lack of confidence—or all of these! It's not true, but it certainly *feels* that way. And worse, we're not sure what to do about it this time—or how to stop it from happening again.

Can you see how reacting to other people's energy over the years might, in fact, be affecting your health—and not in a good way?

SAYING "NO" WHEN YOU MEAN "YES"

Saying "no" doesn't happen quite as often as the opposite, but it does happen. These open centers—the Spleen, Solar Plexus (again), the G, and the Head and Ajna combination—can keep us out of the decisions that we really should have said "*yes*" to, as we wanted to originally. These are the centers where we're more likely to say "no" out of fear, anxiety, or nervousness.

Our "yes" may sound like this:

- Yes, I think I'm ready to look for a new position to grow into.

- Yes, I'd love to be in a committed relationship with you.

- Yes, it may be time to switch careers to the one I've been passionate about for years.

- Yes, I'm ready to step up and out and make a mark with my life's purpose.

Saying "yes" takes courage. And there are plenty of places in the chart where our Strategy will be saying "yes" while our mind or our voice is saying "no." We think there's safety in saying "no." But when it comes to our health, it may be short-lived safety. Eventually, saying "no" to all the places where we can grow is what makes us sick—literally.

Let's take a look at those open centers that bring up the fears and keep us in the status quo in the short term.

The open Spleen is all about survival and ways to keep us safe. It's very intuitive by nature and also very attuned to the subtle changes in your health. You'll notice, for example, when you have a scratchy throat indicating the start of a cold and do whatever you do to prevent it, if possible. It's a great little warning device. When we meet someone that we immediately like, that's our Spleen telling us that this person is funny or nice or safe for us to talk with. When we meet someone whom we decide we'd rather *not* talk to, that's our Spleen telling us that there is something unsafe about this person.

Subtle, but very distinct messages, right?

But it's also the center for fears, our own and other people's. With an open Spleen, we certainly have enough fears of our own. Since they're not usually fears about survival, we call these "false fears." Like the fear of failure or success, fear of the future and past, fear of inadequacy.

We can also pick up very easily on the fears of people around us. And as with any open center, we amplify that energy. It's why people with the open Spleen will rarely go to scary movies in the theater. They might be fine at home watching them, but it can be pretty overwhelming to feel the fears of the entire audience. Feeling your own fear or others' fears can easily make us say "no" in certain situations. We think that "no" will assure safety in whatever form we're hoping to get it. It keeps us safe from risks. And we wonder how much the risk will cost us. It's the "yes" that helps us to grow, and we know that. But we hold ourselves back with the "no," and it feels comfortable.

With the open Solar Plexus, we're picking up on other people's emotions, but also feeling our own nervousness about a situation and, meanwhile, picking up on others' nervousness. A tricky dance. With the open Head and Ajna (about half the population), our openness is literally getting in the way of doing what our Strategy knows is right for us. You can come up with all kinds of great excuses—most rooted in the anxiety of the Ajna—that sound like perfectly legitimate reasons for waiting on something you'd really like to do.

Most of us are quite accomplished at lists of "Pros and Cons." Those are all in the Head/Ajna as the result of our own anxieties, but also the anxieties that others put on us. Whether we acquiesce to our own anxieties or those of our well-meaning parents, spouse, or friends, it's still a "no" that really wanted to be a "yes." Their fears become our fears, and we never take a step forward unless it's assured, safe, and comfortable.

Finally, the open G will have us saying "no" when we'd really like to say "yes" in situations when we are questioning our sense of self. The G is all about our Self—our self-direction and our self-love. Taking a big step into a new relationship or a new position, or even moving to a new location, can be difficult for the open G Center.

With so many ways to jeopardize our decision-making, it's a wonder we ever make a decision that's really in our best interests and following our Strategy. But eventually we do, and that's what keeps us healthy.

Here's something most of us realize when we're in the hospital or in some other acute situation in life: No one can take care of you except you. (Sorry for the bluntness, but we're talking life and death situations here.) No one can take your place with your kids or your spouse when you're healthy—or take your place in a hospital bed when you're ill. And no one can take care of your health except for you. It's up to you. And only you.

How Human Design can help you feel better

The Goals for Health

What are your goals for health? My goal is now health and vitality.

It used to be a lot more complicated. It doesn't have to be.
All I want now is a sense of well-being that allows me to do my work, travel as needed, do all the things we like to do for fun and relaxation, and feel good while I'm doing all of that. Oh…and I want it to continue until I'm done with my life's work—which will probably take till about 110 years old. That should be a good run.

Those are my intentions…and most days that's the reality. I'm very grateful for the health I have now.

But it wasn't always like this. I've lived through the burnout—a few times—the adrenal fatigue, hypothyroidism, a car accident, a cardiomyopathy event (not a heart attack, just a severe panic attack that caused temporary heart muscle damage) that led to a catheterization after four days in the hospital, years of New York City stress, infertility, and bouts of depression. Oh, and the physical body stuff like arthritis of the knees and scoliosis.

Nothing major, really. Just lots of inconvenient and sometimes painful stuff that probably would have been avoided if I had been following my Strategy earlier on.

I hope that following your Strategy and aligning with your purpose makes sense by now—for your ongoing health and well-being—so that you can have the vitality you need to accomplish your goals and dreams. When you are aligned with your purpose, saying what you mean (yes, no, or something in between), and speaking your truth more often than not, you'll be feeling vital, alive, and on purpose.
So let's talk about the concrete steps you can take to keep your body happy while you're doing what makes you happy.

Finding a Plan That Works for Your Strategy

Finding an Eating, Sleeping, and Exercise Plan that works for your Body

If you're under forty, you can read this section and tuck it away for future reference. I'm not really preaching to you yet. Most likely, you fall into one of two camps: you've either found a way that works for you so that you feel healthy *or* you're still feeling superhuman and haven't had the slightest need to tune into your physicality yet. Ah, to be young again!

For those who are over forty, this one's for you! Your physical body starts to change around the time you turn forty. That's nothing new, I'm sure.

From what I've seen as I've coached so many with their Human Design, you can follow a plan that's unique to you and your body and your Energy Type that will keep you healthy and vital for a long time. But it really helps to figure out this ongoing plan between forty and fifty, if you can. Any time is a good time, but if you can begin the steps to finding your own unique way of eating, sleeping, and exercising, it will really serve you in the long run.

What you're looking for is consistency: a way to eat that feels good for you and keeps you at a fit weight for your body type; a way to exercise that you enjoy and that uses up all your daily energy so that you sleep well; and a sleep schedule that rejuvenates you each night. Like most other things in Human Design, this plan is unique to you. So I really can't tell you exactly what is best for you. But I can give you some guidelines:

1. **Eating:** Many of my clients are experiencing new ways of eating, generally because of food sensitivities. Experiment with what works best for you. Like other things in Human Design, your body knows better than you do most of the time. So ask it. Experiment with different foods, avoiding certain foods and sticking to a plan as much as possible so that your body gets used to it. Some people need to stay on the plan one hundred percent of the time; some ninety percent with a little cheating; others can be even more lenient. And please honor the little ones' needs as much as possible. Given the option, their bodies crave what they need.

2. **Exercising:** Exercise programs vary more by Energy Type: Generator types need more exercise each day than non-Sacral types so that they can run out their Sacral energy and sleep well each night. If you have more than one Motor, and especially if you have all four Motors defined (Sacral, Will, Root, and SP), you **must** exercise each day until all the Motors have run out (this includes physical work and running around after children, of course). Projectors and Manifestors don't need to exercise as much without the Sacral, which is the biggest and most consistent of the Motors. Each type should be doing exercise they enjoy so that they will be motivated to do it as needed.

3. **Sleeping:** Most people should be sleeping seven to nine hours per night, according to most scientific articles and Arianna Huffington's book, *Sleep*. You may think you need less, but it's rarely true. When I worked at International Management Group in New York in the early 1980s, the CEO, Mark McCormack, famously bragged that he only needed five hours' sleep a night and worked and traveled most of his waking hours. He had an assistant

in each office (about fifteen at that point), and they had a hard time keeping up with him. Most people did. Unfortunately, he passed away in 2003 at age seventy-two. Some people like the alpha routine; some don't. Find a sleep schedule that works for you and stick to it. If you, like many, are already sleep-deprived, try adding fifteen minutes per day or week to your sleep time until you wake feeling rested and alert. For most sleep-deprived people, the catch-up time will take a while. And yes, you deserve it. Projectors should be getting more sleep on a regular basis—usually up to ten hours, when possible, or a nap if you can. You deserve it, too.

If you can get a plan for these three pieces of your life, and get to a point where they come naturally and they make you feel great, then you've won the battle. Think of these three steps as part of a new health regimen that doesn't need to cost you any more, but can add years to your life. Happy years at that…so that you go out like a candle.

If you are feeling like these suggestions are extreme or would be difficult to achieve with your crazy schedule, kids to worry about, stress at work, and/or troubles in your relationship, then that's exactly WHY you should be reading this. And I ask you to consider the following surrender experiment…

My Surrender Experiment(s)

What is surrender?

Is it giving up, giving in, acceptance, rejection, none of those, or all of those?

I recently read a book called *The Surrender Experiment: My Journey into Life's Perfection* by Michael A. Singer. He is an author and expert on meditation but also has had a very successful career as a programmer and entrepreneur, becoming the CEO of a billion-dollar public company. Having never heard of him previously, but being highly recommended by a number of people, I wasn't sure what to expect. And read it anyway. That was my first act of surrender in a long while.

As I read more and more, I could see his point. When we allow ourselves to surrender to what we're shown, when we surrender to Life and what it brings us, without resistance, Life can unfold in an almost magical symphony of events! That's the premise of the book, and it sounds almost too good to be true, doesn't it?

Let's face it. This surrender thing doesn't sound all that attractive. But 92% of us are Energy Types (Generators, Manifesting Generators, Projectors and Reflectors) that should have things (think people, places, events, situations) to respond to! And even Manifestors can have stuff just appear before them without going after it, necessarily. So why not surrender to what comes our way? You can think of it as the Law of Attraction at work. If we're attracting it, it must be good for us.

One Caveat: In the book, Singer says that he surrendered to whatever came his way—no matter how personally uncomfortable, financially distressing, or mentally challenging it was. He doesn't suggest—nor would I suggest—"surrendering" to anything that goes against your values, mission, or boundaries of health and safety. Just saying.

So let's talk more about what surrender is—or could be—for you.

Surrender is about total acceptance, lack of resistance, and non-judgment. It's all the traits that Eckhart Tolle explains so eloquently in *A New Earth*. It's about taking our egos out of the equation and, in a way, not questioning how or why this thing showed up in our life. It's really about trust.

Trust in the Source, your Inner Being, your Higher Self, the Universe, or whatever you choose to call that energy that guides us through space at such an incredible rate of speed (estimated at close to a thousand miles/hour) that we don't even know we're moving! Yes, we are just tiny little dots on this big green-and-blue planet called Earth, but there is a plan for each of us. And if we'll just let go and receive all the gifts coming our way as we trust that all our needs will be provided for, ultimately the surprises will be there for us—some with bows on. And some without! If we expect that the good stuff will come our way, it will. Sounds like I've got my Pollyanna hat on again, right?

Well, I say that because we're in an age with lots and lots of energy coming in and surrounding us, empowering us, and yes, uplifting us, that will allow your wishes and desires to happen even more quickly than you realize.

As we'll talk about in an upcoming chapter, by the way, making a list of what you want with clarity (or meditating, journaling, etc., in conjunction with making a list) will allow what you want to come even more quickly.

As I got deeper into the book, I realized that I too had been practicing surrender—but only for short periods of time when I really wanted something or needed a change. I called it my periods of "saying yes to everything." (This was years before Shonda Rhimes' book!) Pretty simple. I would just "say yes" to any opportunity I was presented, no matter how crazy, uncomfortable, or weird it seemed. And let me clarify, as I understand it better now. While I was "saying yes to everything," I wasn't going against my gut or Sacral—my gut was approving of it, too. But I was disregarding wholeheartedly my instincts—fearful, distrusting, or uncomfortable as they were.

So one time that I decided to "say yes" was when I decided it was time to get married. I had dated a lot in my twenties but got disillusioned around thirty-two without a soul mate in sight. I took a long break from dating, and when I re-emerged, I just decided it was time and started "saying yes" to every invitation that appeared.

I do consider myself fortunate, lucky, and totally blessed to have found my wonderful husband during that period. But in retrospect, I don't think it was an accident!

Other times I "surrendered" were when we were looking for our current home and the move from NJ that entailed, looking for a job again after our adoption plans didn't work out, and taking on Human Design as a business while still working full-time in Corporate America. Lots of surrender to the powers that be, but also lots of growth, education, fulfillment, and joy!

Looking back, some of those "yes's" seem crazy even now, but they all worked out, and I wouldn't change a thing!

So looking at what's on your plate, what can you surrender to? What can you focus on, remove your ego from, and trust that it wouldn't be there if you hadn't asked for it, if it wasn't a purposeful step on your journey? Those stepping stones are put there for a reason. Trust your steps along the way. Surrender to them. And see what happens. It will be good for your peace of mind and for your health overall.

I felt like I should include Jane Fonda as the health chapter's celebrity profile, since I remember watching her videos in the '80s religiously as the fitness craze hit the States. She's still going strong in her 80s with a new movie and TV series. As Generators, we're both still exercising!

Celebrity Profile

Jane Fonda
Birth Info: December 21, 1937, at 9:14am in New York, NY

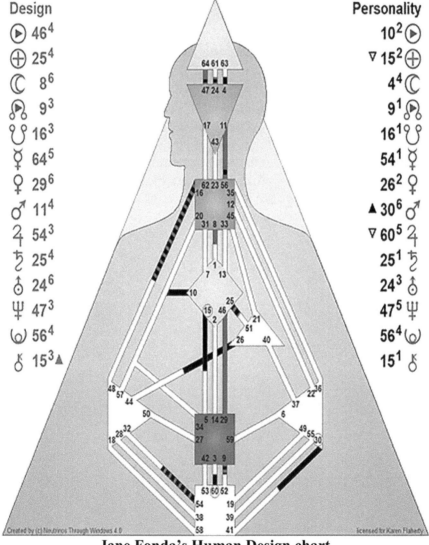

Design

- ▶ 46^4
- ⊕ 25^4
- ☾ 8^6
- ☊ 9^3
- ☋ 16^3
- ☿ 64^5
- ♀ 29^6
- ♂ 11^4
- ♃ 54^3
- ♄ 25^4
- ⚷ 24^6
- ♆ 47^3
- ☋ 56^4
- ⚷ 15^3 ▲

Personality

- 10^2 ▶
- ▽ 15^2 ⊕
- 4^4 ☾
- 9^1 ☊
- 16^1 ☋
- 54^1 ☿
- 26^2 ♀
- ▲ 30^6 ♂
- ▽ 60^5 ♃
- 25^1 ♄
- 24^3 ⚷
- 47^5 ♆
- 56^4 ☋
- 15^1 ⚷

Jane Fonda's Human Design chart

As an actress, activist, fitness guru, model, and author, Jane Fonda has had the kind of life that would seem a whirlwind to many of us! As a Generator with a 2/4 Hermit Opportunist profile, she seems to have taken it all in stride—although with over a million pictures taken of her over the years, one could hardly say that she's the typical "hermit." As the daughter of Henry Fonda, she was in the public eye from an early age, and the Opportunist had a chance to play its role with access to her father's contacts in the movie industry, the ability to travel, and a quick mind.

There are a few themes that have played out in her life as her defined channels:

The 64-47 is the Channel of Abstraction. With the defined Head and Ajna, Jane was an inspiration and would likely receive information in a uniquely abstract way. She would see the big ideas long before her peers and had the abstract thoughts that kept people intrigued.

The 11-56 is the Channel of Curiosity and is also called the channel of the "Seeker"—as in always trying to explore the unknown. With both ideas and the gift of storytelling, Jane was able to keep up with the best of them in all walks of life. She would take on the big ideas, creating a relevant story for her audience, whether through acting, writing, or speaking.

The 29-46 is the Channel of Discovery. It's also called "Succeeding where others fail" because it's comprised of the gates of Commitment, Perseverance, and Determination. Jane's commitment to becoming excellent at each career she took on made it look easy to others. But she worked very hard to achieve her goals.

And just as important as those themes of Discovery, Abstraction, and Curiosity is the fact that Jane Fonda's Incarnation Cross is the Cross of the Vessel of Love. This indicates that her whole raison d'etre is about Love—love of self, love of humanity, love of the spirit, and love of the flesh. People with this Incarnation Cross have a hard time understanding why others can be harsh, why there are wars, and why we can't all just agree to get along. The realities of our lives can seem very odd to the Vessel of Love, and perhaps Jane got caught up in some of these mixed emotions as she trod through a life filled with many different characters—both on screen and off!

Can you see how speaking your truth each and every day—gently but powerfully—would be better for your health and well-being than stuffing down those words, emotions, thoughts, and feelings for days, months, and years? Those are the ultimate causes of any disease. I'm not advocating for anger in the streets here. We could all do with a little more talking and listening, understanding, a willingness to change our minds, and yes, sometimes compromise.

Speaking of compromise, in the next chapter we'll be talking about Parenting Your Children. Who does the compromising in your home?

Chapter 4
Parenting Your Children

Most Common Issues in Parenting

"From the moment that you came into the world, your parents began the conditioning process. Remember, this is not about blame. They didn't know any better. And in that moment of conditioning, there are always those boundaries that are being established about where you can go with that. You've got to walk when they want you to walk, and talk when they want you to talk, and God forbid, you don't do it on time, according to somebody. And that you have to be able to achieve at a certain level, and be social at a certain level, and all of these various things. .. And so the children stand in front of the mirror and say they want to be something different. 'I don't want to be me,' they say. But they don't know who the 'me' is because they're immediately conditioned from the time they come into the world and the conditioning is pounded into them. . .Their only opportunity is to be who they are." Ra Uru Hu, 1999.

This chapter hopes to open you to a world that may be quite unfamiliar to you when it comes to your children. Yes, they are the children you love and adore still. But somehow, they've changed now that they're growing up and you don't quite understand why.

The changes cause all kinds of controversy at home, and you probably feel like there must be a better way.

Of course, your aim is to always protect them, but at what cost? Have we gone overboard in protecting them to the point that they're not feeling free enough to express their unique individuality? My intention is to walk you through how to look at this a little differently so you can gain more understanding, more peace, and more joy at home with your family!

When it comes to parenting these days, it's really not for the faint of heart. Do any of these feelings or accompanying situations describe you with your children?

- Why do I feel like our family doesn't look like what I expected?
➢ Divorces, deaths, step-family of all kinds, piercings, tattoos, and man-buns

- We did the best we could, but what changed?
➢ Technology, drug and alcohol use and abuse, suicides, gun violence

- Why won't they listen to me and do what I say?
➢ Competition at school, cyberbullying, humiliation, physical/sexual harassment, lack of family engagement

- Why does he/she want to be a creative, when I'm an accountant? (or vice versa!)
➢ Personal individuality that bucks family traditions, isolation, hostility, anger, and frustration

Human Design was created for the children. Ra always said that. The basic idea is that if we can raise our children according to their Energy Type, Strategy, and Authority, they will be living their authentic selves and not trying to be anything that doesn't feel good to them as growing humans.

It's not easy raising little people. They can be so different from their parents. Just imagine two Generators raising two Projectors. Or the opposite—two Projectors raising two Generator types. Yikes! Things can get a little dicey.

How can you *know* what's best for your own children?

Answer: Once you understand your own Strategy and definition, you can then start to understand *their* definition and know their Strategy and Authority. It's one of those things that sounds simple, but it's not necessarily easy.

The issues that most parents tell me they run into fall into a few categories. The biggest one is: "What's wrong with my children?" A lot of parents have the expectation that their children will look and act like "mini-me's." They may *look* like one parent or the other, but their actions—even if they are the same Energy Type as one parent—may be incredibly different, or at least should be. And yet, this is where our conditioning starts. At the very beginning.

Nature vs. Nurture

This is actually a good place to talk about conditioning. It starts when we are very small. Our parents expect us to act a certain way—like them. And sometimes, the child will have definition in their chart that *does* look like one of their parents. But many times, it's quite a different configuration. In fact, most children have charts that look more like one or more of their grandparents' charts. That's a story for another day, but a very interesting one to see when you run all the grandparents' charts. It's a generational thing—where the energetic blueprint and genetics actually skip a generation.

The definition (their defined or colored-in energy centers) that a child has in their chart is the way they are really here to act or to be. Let's think of that as their Nature. The Energy Centers that are defined for your child are the ones that are consistent for them; it's how they're wired. That's the way they *want* to act out their personality. But they don't live in a vacuum. They live with parents and siblings who have different centers defined.

The Energy Centers that are open on their charts are the places they take in energy from their parents. They not only take it in, but they also amplify it. As a result, the child takes in those particular energies all the time and *thinks* that is their energy. Let's think of that as Nurture. (A group of college students first asked me about Nature vs. Nurture, and I've never forgotten it. It was a profound question!)

The child may have a parent with the Will Center defined, for example, while the child's Will Center is not defined—it's open. But after only a short time of taking in that energy at home, the child *thinks* they have that willpower energy. They think they can do anything. They feel good around their parents and feel empowered to do what their parents want them to do. But as soon as the parent goes out of the room to do something else, the child wonders why they don't feel the same way. And they decide to do something else. It doesn't seem as important to do their homework or clean their room after their parent leaves.

One of my clients has a Will Center, but none of her children do. She was amused to realize after our session that in fact her children *only* did chores when she was around. The children feel empowered when their mother is with them, but then that energy goes away. And unconsciously, they do wonder where it's gone. The irony is that the children will feel like the willpower is theirs, even if it is inconsistent. Most of my clients are relieved to hear that they don't actually have willpower after a lifetime of wondering why it's evasive. That is how conditioning works. Does that sound familiar?

On the other hand, a child with a Will Center may run circles around parents who don't have the Will Center defined. The child may want to go out for every sport, join every club, and push themselves to do well in school. By middle school, parents don't mind this behavior as much, but it starts out as a willful child who doesn't want to go to school at all or eat their peas and carrots or say "hello" to a neighbor.

Are the variations in energies beginning to make more sense now? Can you see how one household with four people can become the Wild West when so many different combinations of energies are playing out?

As we'll see it play out in the work environment, parents feel more comfortable when their children are more like themselves. And children pick up on that quite early on. They try their best to be like their parents, to emulate them, to stay on their good side, and to generally stay out of trouble. But they can only keep that "mask" on for so long. By the time they are ten to twelve years old, they've tired of not being who they really are . This is when the "rebellious behavior" starts to kick in and parents wonder what happened to their lovely, mind-melded, well-behaved children.

"What's wrong with them—why have they changed so much? It must be a phase—I hope it's a phase!"

Please don't shoot the messenger, but there's nothing wrong with them!

You tried to raise them the best that you could. You may have even tried to raise them as your parents raised you—or, in your own act of rebellion, the opposite of that.

But they are quite different from you. They are their own people with their own Human Design charts, and they have a purpose to live out. The children born now (and any children born after 1987) are here to live out their life's purpose immediately. They're actually *not* waiting for anything. And many of them are not even allowing the conditioning from their homes to affect them as much as it may have in the past. These kids—whether you refer to them as enlightened, woke, or on purpose—are here to make a difference. And personally, I welcome them with open arms!

Here's what the kids being born today DON'T need:

- They don't need "helicopter parents." They need independence—within reason, of course.
- They don't need parents who do everything for them. They need to learn how to do things on their own. This is now commonly referred to as "adult-ing" because many young adults have no idea how to do that.

- They don't need to be raised as you were raised. These are very interesting times, but very different times indeed, from your childhood days.

- They don't need to be raised in *fear*. They are fearless beings, and they are repelled by the fearfulness in their parents and grandparents, teachers, coaches, and family friends.

- They don't need to be raised with your conditioning. They are here to be themselves, as they were created from the very beginning.

- They don't need to be forced to learn in school. They will learn much more organically by experiencing what they're motivated to dive into, according to what feels correct for them.

- They don't need to be taught how to learn—each child has their own learning style. They need to discover their own learning style—either on their own or with the guidance of parents or teachers.

We'll discuss these situations when we get to the Solutions part of this chapter. But first, I want to interject the possibility of fear in parenting. It's totally normal and happens to most of us. Parenting is never an easy role, but when children smell fear, they've won the battle. It's not a contest, as you've probably realized. It's not a zero-sum game. When you lose as parents, everyone loses. So it would really be better if some of the fears you have—again totally understandable, no judgment here—were gone or at least dissipated somewhat. So is it okay if we discuss the difference between fear and trust in general and how it might apply to parenting?

The Basics: Fear vs. Trust

One morning, I was watching the Sun rise on the longest day of the year. It's the first day of Summer for many; it's also the day of the Summer Solstice. And as the Sun rises gracefully, majestically, assuredly as a big orange ball over the ocean on the horizon, I can't help but look at it. It's compelling. I know I'm not supposed to stare or even watch too much. But that makes it all the more alluring, doesn't it?

It only took a few minutes to rise above the horizon, becoming a little smaller in the sky then as it rose. And now it's fully ablaze. No clouds or haze to distract. Now the Sun *is* too bright to look at, and I avert my eyes. And it's getting warmer inside already just with a few minutes of Florida Sun on the glass. Wow! The Sun is powerful. Thank goodness for this wonderful, energetic solar power we can depend on day after day to light our way and warm the planet and provide nutrients for our plants and ourselves. What would we do without it?

In fact, has it ever occurred to you that the Sun may *not* rise one morning?

Probably not.

We kind of know, as Annie says, that "the Sun will come out tomorrow." Or as the Beatles sang, "Here comes the Sun." Probably two of the most optimistic songs ever written, right?

So we can agree that we kind of trust that the Sun will be there each and every day. That's reassuring; it's a constant. We have no control over it, but we do know and trust that it will be there each day. And it feels good to know that.
Good vibrations!
I've been thinking about fear lately—since I did an interview for a telesummit. So what if we're in fear, feeling fear for some reason? I was wondering if we can feel trust *and* fear at the same time? Can we hold both feelings at once? I'm thinking, "No," but let's think this through.

Are they opposites? Like light and dark? A smile and a frown? Up and down?

Abraham-Hicks, as they talk about the Law of Attraction, says that *fear* is the lowest vibration we can have. And at the other end of the spectrum there are feelings like joy, love, gratitude, trust. So yes, it would seem that they are at opposite ends of the vibrational-feeling spectrum.

So how do we get from one end to the other? How do we let go of fear and get to that better-feeling place?

Well, there are lots of ways, and I would gently suggest that the easiest way is to find your way to gratitude for something in your life. This is an exercise I suggest to my clients all the time.

If fear is the lowest vibration we can have, then gratitude is the highest. And it's pretty easy to find something that you're grateful for, I suspect. If it's not that easy, then take a few very deep breaths (perhaps count to ten!), and then think of something to be grateful for. And do that until you get there! It's worth it! Whether you write it down in a Gratitude Journal, meditate on it for a while, walk in nature, or just gaze upon your child as they sleep, each of these actions will bring you to gratitude and better feelings overall.

As we relate this to parenting, you may already be thinking: "Of course I love my children unconditionally. But they're SO frustrating!"

We're evolving so quickly now, the energies are also moving quickly and a lot of our vibrational status quo has shifted and changed. Just look at the news around us. How does this affect our families?

All of these changes are causing stress and upset and fears to show up in us even when we may have thought that they were under control. Each of us, we've done *so* much over the past few years— and maybe even decades—to control our fears, give them up to other higher feelings, and yet there they are again! Do you wonder if we'll ever get to the point where we won't need another lesson?

And yet the fears show up in family situations all the time. From what I see and hear, parents are fearful quite a bit, actually. You're fearful the children will get hurt or sick from an early age, even when you're generally in complete control of their surroundings. What could possibly happen when they're nestled in their crib, fully taken care of, all swaddled and sleeping? "Lots!" you may have thought. Then as they grow, the possibilities for playing outside, at the playground, at school, with friends or bullies, make parents nervous, worried, and anxious. I get it. It happens all the time. And I'm not going to say it will go away. (Heck, I still worry about the two foster children we had for a year—and that was years ago!) The worry never really leaves you.

What if you could dial down the worry and anxiety and nervousness, and teach your children that you trust that they'll be okay? At least a little. That you have a deep knowing that they'll be watched over, taken care of, and provided for? (It doesn't really matter if you believe that it's God, the Universe, the community, or friends and family who will provide, as long as you don't feel like it's *only* your responsibility. Ultimately, it is, of course, but it's nice to **trust** that there is other help along the way.) That when they step out of the house each morning, they will return as happy, healthy, educated children on the way to being adults.

I suspect that if you're reading up to this point, you're at least familiar with and perhaps practicing the Law of Attraction for yourself. That you've accepted full responsibility for your life and your actions, and you're moving forward with your goals and intentions. Or you're on your way to that understanding. And, with a little persistence, it seems to be working, doesn't it?

So what if you could pass those practices on to your children? To take full responsibility for their life, their actions, and their goals and intentions? And to do it according to their Strategy and design, just as you are beginning to? What if you could let go of the labels we have for children, let go of all the "bad stuff" in the news that happens to a very, very small percentage of children, let go of the limiting beliefs and fears that don't describe the future you want for yourself or for your children?

As an extreme example of changing one feeling to another, a real transformation took place following the murders of nine congregants in Charleston, SC, at the Emanuel A.M.E. Church in 2015. If the people of Charleston and the families of those who were killed can look at the suspected killer in court and forgive him, express love and understanding, and begin the healing process, what can the rest of us learn from this? If out of such hatred can come some good feelings and forgiveness and love—when things could have gone in a different direction—don't these generous people become our teachers?

If we look beyond the "bad stuff" that's happening and look for the good just beyond it, it's a lot easier to deal with on a daily basis. There are so many more good people in the world than not. There are so many more people who prayed or went to church or celebrated with their families today than didn't. When our focus is on the "good," the "bad" has no choice but to diminish in our view. Don't give your power or thoughts to the stresses, fears, and upsets of the world. We need to give our thoughts to the good thoughts! You always get to choose your own reality. Discover your powers. Anchor your energy. Take care of you first—to be able to do what you're here to do.

The choice is yours. The choice is always yours.

Goals

So in a perfect world, how would parents and children act with each other? What is the ultimate goal?

When Ra Uru Hu created the Human Design System in 1987, as I mentioned, it was created for the children. His idea was that by letting the adults—mostly mothers—know about Human Design over the past thirty years, the beauty, simplicity, and pragmatism of Human Design would trickle down to their children. And their children ... and their children ... and so on. Many thousands and perhaps millions of people have heard about Human Design, got to know their chart better, and told their friends and families about it. While it's still a relative "secret," I'm meeting more and more people who have already heard of Human Design at shows and conferences and online. The word is definitely spreading.

Why was Ra so insistent this system be taught to the children by their parents? He wanted the parents to embrace it first, live their Strategy, and be an example to their children as they lived their Strategy. He was envisioning an idyllic world—patiently but expectantly. Like a proud father himself, he was expecting Human Design to be at the forefront of the birthing of a new planet—a new Earth and perhaps even a Heaven on Earth, as some lightworkers envision. Ra's vision was of a happy, healthy, vibrant world where each individual is embracing Human Design and living out their Strategy so that each of us fits perfectly into the puzzle of humanity—each of us playing the role that we came forward to play.

Now that Ra has passed away, I hold that vision, as do many of my teachers and colleagues in the Human Design community—and in increasing numbers, my clients. It's very exciting!

It's a beautiful thing to see someone's potential in their chart, show them the genius that's been there all along and have the light bulb turn on! To hear the "a-ha" moment and to realize that they'll never look at themselves as they did before ever again. The potential for wisdom, creativity, peace, and love are all there—not only for you, but for your children, family, and friends. After all, Human Design *was* created for the children. I know that they're ready to hear it. The little ones are ready for this—they're waiting for us to catch up!

Solutions

Some Solutions to Mindful Parenting

We've already talked about the concepts of Nature vs. Nurture and raising your children with enough independence to allow them to be themselves. Additional points to make about being mindful when it comes to parenting in relation to Human Design include details about understanding the specific Energy Centers that are defined and that can cause challenges around their Strategy, lovability, and learning styles.

Understanding Your Child's Human Design Energy Type and Strategy

It is important to understand your own Human Design and use your Strategy, and then as each child is born, or as you learn about their Human Design, start applying their Strategy to every decision you make for them. This will help them to model that decision-making behavior for themselves as they get older. For example, if you have a young Projector, invite them into activities at home or on the kplayground so that they get into the habit of receiving and deciding upon invitations that they get. For your Generator-type children, keep asking them lots of yes and no questions so that they can practice responding to your questions or requests. And for your Manifestor child, give them enough space to be themselves. The Manifestor child can have some freedom, but they should always inform you what they're up to and where they're going and with whom.

Raising Them With Your Principles And Love (G Center)

Children with the open G Center are especially prone to feeling like they are not lovable. Not so much that *you* don't love them, but that in general they're not as lovable compared with the other children. The child with the defined G Center will have a fairly consistent feeling about their direction in life and their sense of being lovable. The open G will not. And this will be a feeling they have throughout their life. Their direction for career, schooling, and friends may be quite changeable. But they get along with everyone because that openness makes them like chameleons. They can be with all types of friends and really enjoy their company, because they understand those friends at a deep level. But because they question their lovability, they will need a lot more reassurance of your love than defined G kids.

About half the population has a defined G Center. This energy feels like you have a good sense of self, your direction in life, and love of the self. It's a very solid kind of energy. But the open G Center is here to know others. They have a sense of being changeable depending on who's around them—someone who could befriend almost anyone with a very diverse circle of friends. With an open G Center, these kids can become great therapists, teachers, counselors, and coaches. They can literally "see" into someone's soul, help them with any problem and usually give very sage advice. They're not here to know themselves as much as they are here to know others.

The best way to have open G kids feel like they are loved and have a sense of direction is to make sure that they're comfortable in their home, school, or wherever they hang out a lot. This will sound strange, but you likely know your child: Location is very important for them and for finding their direction in life. You may have already noticed this behavior in them, and if you haven't, then ask them about it. They are just much happier when they are in a place where they feel comfortable. There's probably a favorite corner of the house they like, or a restaurant, or one or more of their classrooms at school. Ask them!

Hopefully, the places they're in the most often are comfortable energetically for them. Have they ever told you some restaurant just doesn't feel right to them? It's easy enough to go to another restaurant or change tables. Sometimes at home, you can move the furniture in their rooms around—or let them do it. You may not have as many options at school, but again it could be as simple as moving their desk to another part of the room.

This is one of those funny-sounding explanations that can make a world of difference to your child. One client had a Manifestor boy child who changed pre-schools at eighteen months and stopped talking once he got to the new school. They had thought he was autistic until they moved again and put him in a special-needs kindergarten. Once there, he started talking in complete sentences and hasn't stopped. With his open G, once he was in a comfortable place that he really liked, he began to thrive and is no longer considered autistic.

Encouraging Your Children To Find Their Own Learning Style

The Head and Ajna are the two triangles at the top of the body graph on your child's chart. If the Head and the Ajna are open, then your child will have a unique learning style. If their Head and/or Ajna are defined, they may have their own learning style, but they will be much more likely to fit into any school environment easily. The defined Ajna children find it easy to memorize, learn facts and figures by rote, and will follow instructions, for the most part. They get good grades early on and seem to breeze through their classes and homework.

The open Head and Ajna children are fifty percent of the population, so it's not uncommon at all to have this configuration. Whether they figure out their learning style at home as a toddler or at pre-school, or later on in their schooling, it can make a big difference in how much they learn and how much they enjoy school.

Unfortunately, for many open Head/Ajna children, parents and teachers are unaware of this and usually treat all the children the same. But there's a big difference. I've talked with clients who never figured out their learning style until later in high school or even as college students, or they went back to college when they finally figured it out. What a challenge for them! But what a relief and feeling of accomplishment when they finally received their degree by using their own learning style!

The reason that the open Head/Ajna children have a different learning style is exactly because of the openness up there. It makes things quite busy. They're always taking information in from the people around them, the music they're hearing, a lecture, the TV or a video game, plus all the stuff they've taken in previously and held on to for some reason. They are distracted very easily as a result, and it also makes it hard for them to focus on anything, especially studying.

On the positive side, the open Head/Ajna is very open-minded, can see all sides of any subject, and they ask great questions, when given the opportunity. Some of our most creative minds in history have had open Heads and Ajnas, like Albert Einstein. And he's a great example of someone who didn't find his learning style right away. His teachers thought he would never learn. But once he was encouraged by his mother to find his learning style, his brilliance shone through. Each child needs that time, that opportunity to learn about themselves and find that style. It's much easier, of course, in a private school, but attentive parents can be very helpful also.

These children can have doubts about their intelligence, especially when they are parented by someone with a defined Ajna. Certainty is important to the defined Ajna, whether it's about beliefs, math, or religion. But the open Ajna child cannot be certain in a consistent way. So in order to please the parent, they will act as if they are certain about something to avoid ridicule or embarrassment. This is one of the "Not-Self" behaviors that can be conditioned over time and that is not helpful to the child at all.

Finding their learning style can help both the child and the parents to understand the child better. Any child's learning style can be discovered by working with them, practicing with them, and spending time observing which ways of learning are easiest and most effective. For some, it's very visual; for others, auditory or even kinesthetic. And for many, it's a combination. A number of my clients have told me that some combination of listening to a lecture, writing notes, perhaps re-writing the notes following class, and then studying from those re-interpreted notes proves to be a combination that works for them. That may sound simple, but when these students compare themselves to the defined Ajna kids, who hear things once or read things once and ace the test, it can seem like a lot more steps. And it is, until they find their rhythm. So the sooner they find their learning style, the easier time they will have in school and the happier everyone will be!

Good Vibrations and Great Expectations

We are in a force field of energy, according to quantum physics and Human Design—whether it's love or some other feeling—whenever we're with someone else. Very simply, what happens is that *our* open Energy Centers *feel* their defined Energy Centers, take that energy in and amplify it, and vice versa; their open centers take in our defined centers and amplify them. When you are taking in their energy and amplifying it, especially the emotions of the Solar Plexus, for example, it can feel like *you're* having those feelings or emotions. But you're not really. You're just amplifying the emotions. The same thing happens with each of the other centers.

So as parents, when you're with your children, and all that's around us is energy, you have the capacity to direct that energy. You can take responsibility for your own energy and then encourage the rest of the family to understand and take responsibility for their own energy. You can expect that. You deserve to expect that and so do they. It's what I like to call "Good vibrations." (Do you remember the old Beach Boys song?) You can get to good vibrations over time—there's no rush and there's no deadline—the only requirement is practice. In fact, I love that the song starts with "Wouldn't it be nice....?" That's a phrase that I and so many of my clients use as our way of setting intentions and goals for the future, by asking that question and filling in the end of it with a request. It's a very joyful, carefree, and calm (rather than desperate) but expectant way to make a request of the Universe.

So to end this chapter, what kinds of intentions would you make for your own family in light of what you've just learned?? Things like:

• Wouldn't it be nice if all the kids got better grades this semester?

• Wouldn't it be nice if we had a dinner conversation that was fun, uplifting, and helped one of the kids with an issue they were dealing with?

• Wouldn't it be nice if we started our dinner with each person recounting something that they were grateful for today?

• Wouldn't it be nice if we had a weekend activity planned where everyone could attend?

• Wouldn't it be nice to have some one-on-one time with each child each month and call it our special time?

• Wouldn't it be nice to come to an understanding about why X is so important to my child right now?

There are lots of things you can have intentions for. Make it a habit, if you like. Once you start watching these intentions materialize, it gives you and your children the motivation to ask for more. Ask for more. You and your family deserve it.

One final note: Please don't worry if you've come to the realization that your chart is or isn't particularly tribal or nurturing or whatever. Any design can be a wonderful parent—they come in all shapes and sizes—on the Human Design chart, that is! As always, living out your Human Design Strategy and Authority will lead you on the path to fulfilling your life's purpose and finding your passion in life, along with your children, and in harmony.

Celebrity Profile: Parenting with Tom and Gisele

Tom Brady: Born August 3, 1977, at 11:48am in San Mateo, CA
Gisele Bundchen: Born on July 20, 1980, at 5:00pm in Tres de Maio, Brazil

No matter what you think of their respective but sometimes controversial industries—football and modeling—Tom Brady and Gisele Bundchen are at the top of their game. Tom is the stylishly handsome quarterback of the New England Patriots, has won five Super Bowls, and has been a starter on the team since 2000. His stunningly beautiful wife, Gisele, is an internationally known and recognized model, producer, actress, and businesswoman, who has graced over six-hundred magazine covers in her career so far—second only to Princess Diana.

Together, they make a handsome couple who are not just physically attractive, but also seem to have a happy marriage and home life with their two children, Vivian and Benjamin. They live on an estate in the Brentwood section of LA, and another in Boston, where they grow their own fruits and vegetables for their vegan lifestyle. Sounds idyllic, doesn't it? While we don't know a lot about their parenting style, they do manage to keep their small children protected from the scrutiny of the press, and they seem to model their ideals and philosophies for them by nurturing them with their presence and nourishing them with what they think is best.

Let's look at their charts and see where the magic happens! Both Tom and Gisele are Generators; Gisele has her Emotional Solar Plexus defined and Tom does not. They met on a blind date set up by friends of theirs. And as they say, the rest is history. Was it fate, or was there a spark that just couldn't be ignored? Or both?

If we look at Gisele's chart, we see an Emotional Generator with a lot of open centers—which have the potential to make her a very wise being as she gets older. We're already seeing evidence of this as she manages her career, home life, and philanthropy in a loving and gentle way. She only has two channels defined—the Channels of Reproduction and Mating, and the Channel of Mutation. And her Incarnation Cross is the Cross of Laws. Together, these indicate that she'll be making a difference through her creativity and her children, helping the planet to evolve over the next few decades, but doing it in a way that is observant of the rules and norms of society. She won't be a rabble-rouser—more likely a very vibrant, caring, and committed force for change in the world as she moves the needle on the things that she cares about.

Tom's chart is also quite open, as he only has four centers defined. His channels are the Channels of Talent (the combination of Enthusiasm and Depth) and Rhythm (always being in the flow)— quite a potent combination for a man who makes his living by throwing the ball consistently in just a certain flow during each game. Tom is the "sensitive" one in the relationship with the Gate 19 sitting prominently in his Incarnation Cross. It's the kind of energy that would have Gisele come to his defense when something goes wrong, for example, by protecting her "sensitive" guy when he's hurting. And with the Gate 57, he's also quite Intuitive on the field and in life. Both Tom and Gisele have the Gate 35, the gate of Change, which we've nicknamed the Gate of the Jack of all Trades! It's the kind of energy that allows them to try many different things and be pretty good, if not excellent, at anything they put their minds to. They also both have the Gates of Intuition, Aloneness—which makes them fiercely loyal to each other—and the Gate of Opinions. But they also both have open Heads and Ajnas, so overall they're quite open-minded and likely to come up with very unique answers to any challenges or issues they come across.

If we put their charts together, there are four places in the chart where their gates match up—which we call electro-magnetics, and this is where the magic happens! These happen to be very interesting "hook-ups" in the chart. Together, they've got the Channels of Transmission, Resources, Synthesis, and Beginnings, Middles, and Ends, and they seem to use each of these to great advantage in their relationships and businesses. The Channel of Transmission is also called the Channel of the Salesperson. Tom has the gate of finding the right people, opportunities, business partners, etc., while Gisele has the gate of closing the deals with integrity. Nice!

Then in the Channel of Resources, Gisele has the gate of Abundance—making money—while Tom has the Gate of Allocation of Resources, the energy of figuring out how to save and spend the money. This is always a lovely combination to see in any couple, because it's a tangible result of the synergy of the energies. It's an observable effect, and they seem to be handling this energy quite well. In addition, it's one of the tantric channels!

In the Channel of Synthesis, Tom has that Gate of Sensitivity—including a love of animals and nature—while Gisele has the Gate of Principles. Together this is a very tribal energy that ensures the health of their relationship and allows them to work together on the same causes. It's the kind of energy that helps a spousal business to work for years and years, while other people ask how they can work side by side like that and not fight. This is how.

Finally, in the Channel of Beginnings, Middles, and Ends, Gisele has the energy to get things started and Tom has the gate to get projects finished. You can just imagine Gisele getting ideas for many projects, starting them, and then Tom gently guiding the energy to get them finished. And together, they have the ongoing Generator energy to finish anything that they determine is worth their time and energy.

Overall, these are the Human Design charts of two people who seem happily ensconced in their family and careers who are really meant to be doing exactly what they're doing. It seems like they are following their Strategy as Generators to get exactly what they want for themselves, their immediate and extended families, and their successful business and philanthropic ventures.

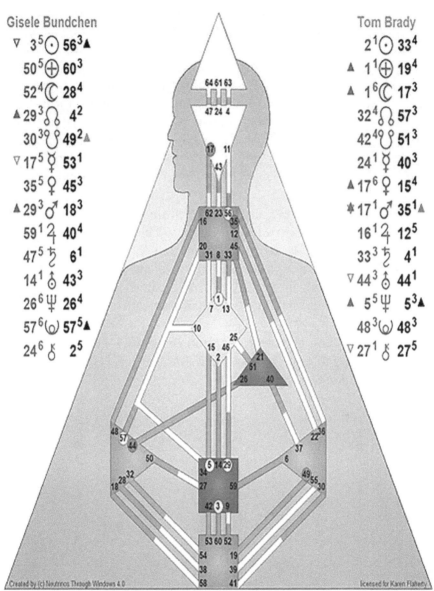

Gisele Bundchen and Tom Brady's composite Human Design chart

When it comes to parenting, one thing I'd like to emphasize is that parents are always doing the best that they can. Whether you're the parent, or you're thinking of your parents in this chapter, they were always doing the best they could for you with what they had and with what they knew at the time. You may know more now and that will help your children. You may have more now, and that may also help children. But those parents who didn't have Google or the technology we have now or the ability to buy us the things we really, really wanted as a kid, they always wanted more for us than they had. And they did the best they could to make that happen with whatever they knew. If they could have done better, they would have. I'm grateful every day for the sacrifices and growth my parents achieved on our behalf. They did the best they could!

Bottom line is: We could all do with a little more Nature and a lot less Nurture in the form of conditioning. This would take a lot of pressure off the parents to figure things out for themselves. With a blueprint for each child, there are a lot less questions about *how* to do things. And a lot more answers. A lot more allowing and a lot less shushing or reprimanding or embarrassment.

Now let's move on to your career and its issues—also created in a greenhouse of parenting by too much Nurture and less than optimal amounts of Nature.

Chapter 5
Your Career

Most Common Career Issues

"Remember that in the moment you meet someone, not only do they put their design in you, you put your design in them. This is how we come together, and it is the nature of life itself....And we will always be attracted to the centers that are open on our charts. We're attracted to what we're not....There is nothing more powerful in the human species than a defined Sacral center. Sacral beings are the great workers of the planet." Ra Uru Hu, 1999.

I would dare to suggest that most of us are living our conditioned selves because our loving families so ingrained in us the principles of doing well, doing good, succeeding as our parents or even beyond our parents, and generally making them proud. All that gentle and not-so-gentle pushing led many of us into careers that we would *not* have chosen for ourselves. Some of these careers are okay; they're not horrible. And some of them pay quite well. But they may not be what we're passionate about.

When I graduated from college, I had already had a number of different jobs, including working for the family tree business since the age of seven (no child labor laws in my day!), internships, and running the Newspaper Agency at Penn for two years as my work-study job, where we delivered about 2,500 newspapers a day around campus. All good experiences for a high-energy Generator child! Working at a young age kept me occupied, instilled a very good work ethic, and helped me understand life's relationship between hard work and money. Coming from a modest background, those were big lessons.

Once I had my degree, I thought things would be a lot easier in terms of finding work that I loved instead of just tolerating it. But no, it wasn't. I went from one job to another pretty quickly in the first ten years of my career: quitting because I'd outgrown the job, getting fired because they'd outgrown me, or looking for other positions because I was bored. They all seemed like the "one" when I started, but I was naïve and still learning the ropes. And while I was a woman thinking that I could do anything I wanted, I started to realize there was no direct path to the corner office.

Now that I know about Human Design, it all makes a lot more sense. As a Generator, I was getting frustrated with the learning curves of each position, which led to premature exits. If I had waited out the frustration, for example, I might have pushed through the lessons and come out with a promotion, rather than another new job. Now I know. But it would have been so much more reassuring if I had known some of this in my twenties. Some of those very challenging times might have been avoided.

Do any of these challenges show up in your life?

- Working/staying in a job that's gone stale. You really loved it when you first started, but now it's going nowhere.

- Looking for a new career or new project—not necessarily looking for security, but more experiences to grow.

- Starting a completely new venture—getting up the resources and courage to make a change.

- Communications among team members, especially in cross-functional/international teams.

- Finding ways to manage stress at the office, in teams and with management.

- Finding your true calling—one that you're passionate about.

- Increasing employee engagement—reportedly at an all-time low right now.

One client recently told me that he had always wanted to be a pilot. He told his father of his dream when he was about sixteen years old. His father, a successful salesman, told him that the only job that will always be there is sales and that flying a plane was not much better than being a bus driver. His dreams were dashed in that moment. So he became a very successful salesman for almost forty years, with some ups and downs, and he was never happy. Around fifty-five, he got his pilot's license, started getting clients, built his own practice at a local airport and now loves what he does every day. He's content, fulfilled, and has the freedom of doing what he's passionate about.

There are so many people who are in careers that they just aren't passionate about. You may be one of them. The lack of passion leads to the rampant lack of engagement in many corporations. It makes sense. If you don't love your job, why would you continue year after year to *pretend* that you're engaged in what you're doing and want to learn more to succeed? That's a hard deception to keep up for too long.

Do we Ever "Graduate" Out of Our Conditioned Selves?

When we hear about graduations, weddings, commencement addresses, and the words of wisdom at all these events, I was wondering if we ever truly "graduate" from the unseemly side of our conditioned selves? To explain, this would be a behavior or attitude that flies in the face of peace, love, and understanding. You know the kinds: a temper tantrum, a resentment that goes on for far too long, gossiping, judgments, lack of acceptance, or just downright mistaken motivations, like trying to gain attention, power, or influence.

In Human Design, Ra Uru Hu (the creator of Human Design) says that we "de-condition" from our conditioned selves after we've known about our Human Design Strategy for about seven years. I'm about nine years into this experiment, and I wonder, after watching others with more experience than me, if we ever get over the triggers that we grew up with? What we mean by "conditioning" is the rules or behaviors or beliefs that we grew up with because of our families', teachers', or friends' influence on us. These are the things like acting out, dramatic emotions, using our head to make decisions, rebelling just because, or taking actions that just don't serve us or even sabotage our intended goals. Why do we do these things—to ourselves and to others? And why is it so hard to get past them, even if you know your Human Design Strategy?

We take these actions that don't serve us because we feel disempowered or angry or inadequate. It's because we perceive an injustice or a slight or an unkind word in our direction. Basically, it's because we perceive that we're different or isolated or just not one of the group. And that feels uncomfortable.

Even though we know our Strategy, and even if we're learning to be more open, kind, loving, accepting of all, it can still be a challenge to *remember* that when we get "triggered" by something. Triggers can include a family member's visit, an event that brings back childhood memories and behaviors, or just a type of food or location or song that recalls a less-than-happy childhood memory.

We can't banish those triggers from our lives, but we can deal with them more effectively so that they have less of an impact on us and those we love. Here's a very powerful tactic for dealing with these triggers that I heard about recently:

- First, identify the trigger: song, location, food, etc. (Rather than just pushing it aside, and "ignoring" it, but allowing it to distract your activity or conversation.)

- Give it a moment in your mind. Realize that it can no longer hurt you, you've got ways to handle it now, and you're not the child you were when it first happened. Talk to yourself, calm yourself, and reassure yourself until it no longer has the jolt it had when you encountered it.

- Tuck it away in your mind as something you've dealt with as an adult, and that you no longer need to give it any "power" over you. And then continue with your activities.

While this seems like a simple exercise, it can be very effective for dealing with those triggers that pop up in the most unexpected ways. Once you've dealt with it, you can resume your life, your activities, and your intended goals in the way that you want!

Fears in The Chart and in Your Career

It's time for you to finally experience the sense of control that you want in your life, without bowing to fear at every corner or decision point at work. It's much better to make peace with the fears that hold us back so that you can get on with your life.

Instead of the world of fears that you've been experiencing, imagine if you could:

- Enter a networking event—where you don't know anyone—and have pleasant and meaningful conversations about your work and what you're passionate about.

- Start business relationships with a firm footing and a real potential for bonding on a deeper level so that you experience growth and fulfillment.

- Decide which business events or marketing processes make sense for you—and which to pass up!—based on your own Strategy.

- Do some of the activities that you've wanted to do in the past but were just plain afraid to attempt!

- Finally break through some of the limiting beliefs that just don't serve you or your family anymore.

Is this you?

Fears turn up in so many places that it's hard to remember where and when they first appeared. Do these sound like familiar fears:

In your career: fears of inadequacy, public speaking, outspoken critics, or self-doubt?

In your relationships: fears of rejection, intimacy, and responsibility?

In your finances: fears of lack, your past mistakes, or fear of the future?

In your business: fears of success or failure, or not finding the right clients or employees or partners?

There are lots of labels for fear. And I don't know about you, but I really hate it when someone puts a label on me that doesn't fit. Personally, I think we should get to choose our own labels. But there's a distinction here. I'm not a doctor or psychiatrist. I'm very visual and logical, and when I can see and name something, it feels very different. Like it's hard to argue with an MRI of your leg and you can see the break, right? Just like that MRI, we can see the fear gates in the chart, see the way the brain operates, and see how you act in relationships. It's so cool when my clients see this themselves and then say, "Yeah, that's the way it works!"

None of us are free from fears. It's all part of being human. When we look at our Human Design, we can see the fears that are unique to us, and this will give you tremendous insight into your personality and how you operate. As Ra says, it will give you a deep relief that there's nothing wrong with you. Fear is to be recognized and understood. So once you are aware of the fears in your chart, and then understand them over time, you'll find ways to step through them so that they're not the problems or blocks that they once were. And they can be appreciated for what they are: ways to keep us safe in new situations.

So here's the cool thing about our fears and Human Design: it's all about energy. My energy vs. your energy. This is a really powerful tool for coaches of all types, and it's powerful to see exactly where your consistent fears are beyond just the five Energy Types that we've talked about. For example, you can look at a chart and it can tell you whether you have a fear of inadequacy—you know, where you don't think you know enough about something or you'll never know enough. Another gate can tell you if you have a fear of the past repeating itself or a fear of the future or a fear of failure. It's all there. And once you have an awareness of those kinds of fears, it helps you to develop new ways of moving through those fears so that you don't get stuck, lost, or paralyzed in energy. Because that's all it is—it's energy and it's not even real in terms of survival. You'll be fine if you just move past it.

Brene Brown's groundbreaking book, *Daring Greatly*, lays out the results of the fears that hold most of back: perfectionism, foreboding joy, and numbing. We never feel like we're good enough, so we try to be perfect. We don't think we deserve joy, so we act like it won't happen for us, and we numb ourselves with some addiction (pick yours: food, alcohol, TV, gambling, etc.). According to Dr. Brown, the antidotes are Practicing Gratitude, appreciating the beauty of the cracks, setting boundaries to find true comfort, and cultivating a spiritual practice.

Mind Steps vs. Sacral Steps

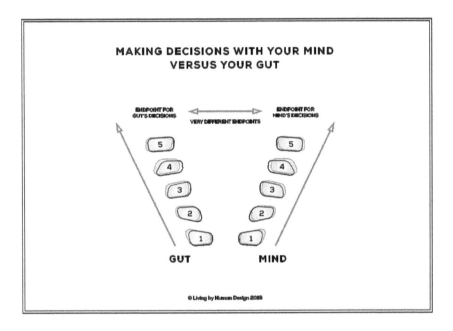

One thing that comes up a lot for Generators and Manifesting Generators (seventy percent of the population) is the challenge of following our Strategy of listening to our gut rather than our head. I get it. We've *all* been raised to check in with our heads before we make any decision. We've been told to "use our head" or figure out the pros and cons of a situation from an early age. But how many times has using your head gotten you into a very sticky situation, and the more you tried, the worse things got? Conversely, how many times have you trusted your gut and then regretted it? Many of us have said, "Oh, I wish I had listened to my gut." But I've never heard anyone say, "Oh, I wish I had listened to my head." Have you??

My suggestion here is to try a little experiment. Put your two index fingers up in front of you. Make believe the right one is your head and move it to the right, to the right, to the right. Now, make believe that your left finger is your gut, and move it to the left, to the left, to the left. Can you see how your two fingers could wind up at very different places, following your head vs. your gut when you're making decisions?

Plus, what happens to many of us is that we get paralyzed once we try to make a decision and it fails or doesn't seem successful at first. So we'll use our head, then our gut, then our head, then our gut. If we're using our two index fingers again for this, you can see how we would feel stuck, almost like we're marching in place, and not getting anywhere. That's completely frustrating—and a huge theme for all Generators. And we hate that feeling. So stop it. Start trusting your Sacral response—your gut—and see what happens. You may be pleasantly surprised!

Goal: Confidence in Self & Trust in the Universe

The goal, of course, is having a career or position that you love and can't wait to get to each day. So many graduation speeches carry these very words, but how many of us actually listen and have a way to accomplish these wise suggestions?

This quote is from the conclusion of Ronan Farrow's Commencement address at Loyola Marymount University in Manhattan in May of 2018:

> So here's what I would say to you. No matter what you choose to do, no matter what direction you go, whether you're a doctor treating refugees or a financier making money off of foreclosures...
>
> And I genuinely hope you don't do that....
> You will face a moment in your career where you have absolutely no idea what to do. Where it will be totally

unclear to you what the right thing is for you, for your family, for your community.

And I hope that in that moment you'll be generous with yourself, but trust that inner voice. Because more than ever we need people to be guided by their own senses of principle—and not the whims of a culture that prizes ambition, and sensationalism, and celebrity, and vulgarity, and doing whatever it takes to win.

Because if enough of you listen to that voice—if enough of you prove that this generation isn't going to make the same mistakes as the one before—then doing the right thing won't seem as rare, or as hard, or as special.

No pressure or anything.

Congratulations, class of 2018.

Solutions

"So, I say to you, forget about the fast lane. If you really want to fly, just harness your power to your passion. Honor your calling. Everybody has one. Trust your heart and success will come to you."
—Oprah Winfrey
#ColumbineClassOf2018

If the goal is having a career or position that you love and can't wait to get to each day, what does that look like?

When you're aligned with what you're here to do, it's actually very attractive. You will radiate an attractive energy that says, "Here I am, World. I got this!" and the World will follow you anywhere. It's that kind of powerful magnetism, that certainty of purpose that's authentic, glowing, and allows you to find your way among strangers.

And unfortunately, when you're not doing what you're here to do, it's pretty much the opposite of attractive.

Understanding your chart allows you to discover the authentic you—the one that feels right to you.

The strategy of "Just Do It" only applies to four percent of the population—just half of the Manifestors. The rest of us have a decision-making Strategy of waiting for something, or waiting out the emotional wave for Manifestors.

That decision-making Strategy is unique to you and allows for free will choices that bring confidence and peace. No more second-guessing yourself. Be honest: How much time do you spend each day second-guessing yourself and the decisions you've made? I know I used to spend a lot of time doing that, and it's such a relief not to do that anymore.

You know that saying in business that we have to know, like, and trust someone in order to feel comfortable working with them?

Human Design is your way to know, like, and trust yourself. You get awareness of your own personality traits and skills. You then trust yourself and your Inner Being because you start using your Strategy. Then you can actually trust the decisions you're making for your career, finances, and in your relationships. Finally, you get to like or love yourself because you understand what makes you tick, what makes you special, and it's pretty easy to see in the chart why you're here. My clients say that they feel *seen* for the first time in their lives.

As always, if you're following your Strategy and Authority to get there, you will eventually get there. Here are a few of the things that usually get in the way, especially at work, and how you can get around them.

The Throat Center:

We covered the Throat a bit in Chapter 2 around relationships. The same applies at the office, of course, but it usually gets much more interesting when so many different types are trying to talk. The Manifestors and Manifesting Generators will have much more opportunity to speak, and because of their attractive Throat energy, people will encourage them to speak more often than other types.

What I suggest to Projectors, Generators, and Reflectors in business situations is that they honor their energy by waiting to speak, but speaking up whenever they are given the opportunity. With people you know, it's not so difficult to be heard and to get your points across. But with strangers or in large crowds, it's much more difficult to be heard.

In a meeting, for example, I suggest waiting to be asked for your opinion or suggestion. I know, that sounds too passive. If you do have something to contribute, I would suggest raising your hand or catching the leader's eye, so that the leader of the meeting sees that you'd like to speak. That works much better than trying to talk over others. Most times, you won't be heard, and if you are, someone else may repeat what you said, but then get the credit for it.

In networking events, I suggest walking into the room, getting something to eat or drink, and then just walking around until you see someone you know or are approached by someone to start a conversation. As you probably already realize, it just doesn't usually work for non-motorized Throats to be the ones to walk around to everyone in the room and introduce themselves to everyone. It's uncomfortable and usually not very fruitful.

Instead of walking in blind, I suggest setting an intention before the event (such as, "I'd like to meet three people who can help with this new project or introduce me to people who can help.") and then letting your energy attract others to you. It just always works so much better, and is easier on your nerves, if you allow others to approach you to start up a chat. Usually, by the way, the people who approach you will usually be the generous match-making

Manifestors and Manifesting Generators who are happy to make introductions to the people they know!

The Root Center: The Root Center is all about adrenal pressure and stress. Two-thirds of the population have this center defined, and as we've said before, these people usually feel quite grounded and stable, and love working with deadlines. And they get a lot done, but on their schedule.

The other third have an open Root Center and feel the stress of the defined Root. They take in that Root energy and amplify it, such that they are the ones who are running around the office, quite stressed that they might miss a deadline. They're the first ones in the office in the morning and the last ones out. They'll work evenings and weekends to try to finish up the tasks that are never-ending. They're rarely calm and would never be thought of as grounded. The solution for open Roots is to stop, take a breath, figure out who or what is causing the stress of the moment, and then, with awareness, figure out what really needs to be done and when. A meditation or yoga practice will also help to calm them.

The Will Center: Only about one-third of the population has a Will Center defined. These are people who are empowering to others, have willpower and a good deal of self-confidence. When we take in their energy of the Will Center, it can feel very empowering to be around them, as if we could accomplish almost anything. We're literally borrowing their willpower for a while. But once we're out of their aura, the willpower goes away, and it makes it harder to accomplish what we promised just moments before. Managers with a defined Will Center will feel like empowering cheerleaders to their employees, saying, for example: "I know you can do whatever you put your mind to!" Of course they can, but when they're away from that Will Center, things just feel more difficult to accomplish. Following your *own* Strategy is the sure way to accomplish any goal, whether you devised it or your manager did.

These are some solutions to the common energy problems that crop up in any office. But I'll suggest that the bigger, overriding question for a lot of working people is: What do I really want, and how do I stay focused on that? Here's where clarity comes in.

Got Clarity??

Asking my clients about their biggest issue around sales and marketing in a survey, it was surprising to get so many that were looking for clarity. No one said "clarity" *exactly*, but that's what it boiled down to.

So "clarity" became a big bucket to put a lot of their issues into, like:

- Where should I find clients?

- What are the right next steps to take?

- How should I be using social media?

- How can I make better decisions so I can sleep better at night?

- How can I find more balance?

- How can I stay motivated?

Marianne Williamson has a beautiful saying:
"The Ego says: Once everything falls into place, then I'll find peace. And the Spirit says: When I find peace, then everything will fall into place."

It's one of those sayings that turns everything we've been taught on its head. I call it an upside-down statement. Or backwards logic.

We're all taught to be logical and to use our heads to make decisions and solve problems. But what if that isn't the best way?

What if there is a better way?

So, back to the survey. I could put each of the answers into groups of things that people want to improve. Groups like: Productivity, Lead Generation, Sales, Social Media, etc. But most of you know *how* to do these things. You've probably had lots of training on them or taken courses before. What's actually lacking is what to do and when.

So rather than put all the answers into those various groups, I'm going to call them all "clarity" as one big catch-all bucket. And here's why.

Each of those "wishes" could be achieved if they were following their Human Design Strategy.

Yes, it's that simple. (Not always easy, but simple.)

Because so many of my clients—after they've had a Human Design analysis done or we've done some coaching around their decision-making Strategy—tell me exactly that. That they have more peace. That all of a sudden, they have more clarity. More clarity about what to do in their business. How to improve their relationships (without changing the *other* person, by the way), how to live their lives in terms of what to eat, and how to sleep and exercise in a way that's best for them.

The most heartening thing to hear is that they've found peace. The kind of inner peace that has you whisper, "Thank you," as you go to sleep and as you awake each morning. The kind of peace that has you laughing more with friends and family and encouraging loved ones and strangers. The kind of peace when you are absorbing just how miraculous nature really is whenever you're lucky enough to be outdoors. The inner peace of knowing that everything is working out for you exactly as it should be, and you don't have to worry about a thing. Your life is occurring in Divine Timing. That kind of peace is priceless.

And, of course, we all revert back sometimes to worry and confusion. We are human, after all! We forget momentarily what we've learned.

Then it's nice to have a reminder to get us back on track. When we remind ourselves to make a list of what we want. Or what we want to change. When a friend reminds us of how special or how (fill in the blank) we are! And then we stop to reflect on the positive rather than the negative. Or we run into resistance and feel the deep frustration of that.

Then finally we stop and wonder: "Why we are making things so damn hard?!" We ask ourselves, "Why don't I just follow my Strategy?" (that is, my Human Design Strategy for making decisions) That would be so much easier!

And then we're back on track. It's just awareness. That was easy!

When we had decided to move to Florida, we kind of knew what we wanted but didn't find anything in the listings that was exactly what we were looking for. And we had been looking a lot! Enough to know what we wanted and what we didn't want. So when we were away for a long weekend, just about a month before we were going down to Florida to meet with some Realtors, we sat on the deck with a drink and made a list. We wrote down just ten things that we wanted in the new condo. Everything from the square footage minimum, HOA fees, and price we wanted to pay (OK, there were a few numbers in there!) to the kinds of people in our community, outdoor activities, and exercise equipment.

When we visited Florida, we saw thirty-seven condos over four days with six different Realtors and drove four hundred miles. After the first day, exhausted but excited, we pulled out our list at a pub and went down the list. I hadn't even looked at the list since the day we wrote it! So imagine how surprised I was to see that not only did the second condo we saw that day have everything on the list, but it was *way better*! I hadn't even imagined a place like we found! It had been on and off the market and had been vacant for over a year. Just waiting for us!

We looked at each other, and since we're both Generators, asked each other, "Do you want to make a bid on this?" and we both came back with "Uh-huh!!" for answers. Our Sacrals knew. We made a bid that night, went on to see the other places, but never found another that matched up to the one we loved. And it all worked out beautifully—quickly, efficiently, the people couldn't have been nicer, and we now are blessed to have had another anniversary in our new home—and we are living our dream!

That clarity got us our dream home, I'm sure of it!

Would you like some clarity, too?

But what if you just don't know what you want? Really. Just don't have any idea and don't know how to get there. What then? How can you get to clarity when you don't know which direction to go in?

Then you've got a few different paths you can go down, and this is the one I always suggest to my clients. I call it the List. It's a list that you create for each area of your life that has ten to twelve items on it that describe that area for you in your ideal. Make a few lists, one for each area of your life that you want to change or improve, for topics like:

- Career/Job or New Venture

- Relationship with Partner

- Family Relationships

- Your Health

- And any other important topic

To do this exercise the first time, get quiet for at least half an hour (whether you meditate, journal, vision board, or do a project plan). And if you think that's too long to spend on creating your new reality with clarity, please just take the time to do it—you deserve it!

Start thinking about what you want. When nothing shows up right away, then think of what you don't want and write down the *opposite* of that. So if you don't like working such long hours, you can write that you have a flexible working schedule that allows for more family time. Or that you have a short commute and lots of time each day to exercise and attend the children's events. Or you have clients and colleagues who are like-minded, friendly, and supportive. It's your list, and you get to make it up as you go along. What can you envision if *your* world was the way *you* wanted it?

One by one write down ten to twelve qualitative descriptions for each area. Don't be *too* specific and just a few numbers, please; the Universe can't abide too many numbers. And don't feel that you have to tackle all the areas at once. Do them as time permits and dreams allow.

Regarding money, I should mention that not one of my clients feels the need to be a millionaire by the end of the year. When my clients get to the income/revenue item, I suggest saying something like: "I make enough money to cover all my business and home expenses, save for the future, invest in the business, and do some of the extra things we'd like to do this year." That usually feels like a contented, but not greedy, order to put in to the Universe!

Once you start thinking about what your world *could* look like, what you envision will feel really great! And that's the way it should feel. That "feeling" place is exactly what will put the Universe in motion to deliver exactly what you've been envisioning. It's like giving an order to a waiter at a fine restaurant. You wait, knowing it will come out beautiful and delicious and even better than you imagined. And no knocking on the kitchen door to ask if it's ready. All your intentions will come to you in Divine Timing, in the same way as your dinner has arrived.

Then it's your choice! You can revisit these intentions daily, weekly, or not at all. Once the "plan" is in place, you don't need to go back to it, unless you want to add something or tweak something.

And yes, I know, this is quite different from your SMART goals, but how long have you been doing those—and have you achieved everything you wanted? I dare to guess that some of the *big* things have eluded you. I'm suggesting an alternative for the *big* dreamy things you want:

- A home life that's peaceful

- A loving relationship with your spouse (and maybe fun and sexy, too!)

- A career that's really fulfilling

- A way to help others

And a word about timing. See, the Universe wants you to have your dreams. If you can just be *very* clear about what you want and then leave the timing to the Universe, you *will* always get what you want.

The Universe will always deliver exactly what you want—and usually even better than what you imagined! The timing will either be sooner or later than you expected, but it will always be the perfect timing for you!

The Universe works its magic for us—each and every one of us—in Divine Timing. So it's always the perfect timing!

If there is something that you would rather be doing or trying on for size, something that you would be more passionate about than your current position, then I would gently persuade you to follow your Strategy to find what it is if you're not sure, and then quietly but diligently find ways to take the courses, get the degrees, or do the research you need to do to be able to move into that career or position as soon as possible. As I always tell my clients, though, don't change just to change. Better to find the resources to be deliberate, focused, and to move into your new profession *without* burning bridges—family or business—in your transition to finding your passionate calling.

Celebrity Profile

Muhammad Ali *(born Cassius Marcellus Clay, Jr.) on January 17, 1942, in Louisville, KY, at 6:35pm;*
Died on June 3, 2016, in Phoenix, AZ.
Manifesting Generator; Profile 1/4 Investigative Opportunist

Whether you refer to him as the "Greatest Sports Figure," the "World Heavyweight Champion" (3 times:1964, 1974 and 1978), the "Sportsman of the Century" (Sports Illustrated Magazine in 1999), the "Most well-known personality in the world," or simply use his nickname, "The Greatest," Muhammad Ali will be remembered by many for a long, long time. After passing away on June 3, 2016, of complications from Parkinson's Disease, from which he suffered since 1984, he had a funeral service fit for a king. And it should be, as he designed the service with his wife, Lonnie, years ago. With speakers that included former president Bill Clinton; Valerie Jarrett; and Bryant Gumbel; comedian and good friend (his "little brother"), Billy Crystal, gave a very heartwarming, uplifting, and humorous eulogy.

The accolades, accomplishments, medals, and awards are probably well-known already. Muhammad Ali lived a full life that started out with boxing, won as an Olympic athlete and then as a winning contender, continued during a break in his career as a political activist, went back to boxing, and finished up as a philanthropist, activist speaker, writer, singer, and even a Broadway and film actor! He was known as one of the quickest heavyweights in history, and his speed never let up, even as he became more and more affected by Parkinson's. After his retirement from boxing, he devoted his life to charitable works, and traveled up to two hundred days a year.

As a Manifesting Generator, none of the above accomplishments are a surprise. He just kept going and going and going. Even as he was banned from boxing for over three years during a prime time of his career, he continued training and began speaking at college campuses about the Vietnam War to support himself and to advance his political and religious agendas.

His only open center was the G Center. All the others were defined, and undoubtedly, made him a force to be reckoned with. Imagine if he had known how powerful his energetic chart was, in addition to his outsized personality and physical beauty! He had a very sharp mind, four very active Motors, including the Will (Ego), and a Throat energy that could be heard from anywhere! He was emotional, but it was a mild emotional wave, since it was Tribal. It's no surprise that the channel which connected to his Solar Plexus was the Channel of Synthesis—a combination of the Gate 19 (Sensitivity) and the Gate 49 (Principles/Revolution). His stand about the draft during the Vietnam War was a principled one. He said, "I got no quarrel with them VietCong." His speeches led to a revolution of both anti-war and racial equality sentiments at colleges around the country.

One of the most intriguing aspects of his personality was his ability to speak in a way that the press and his fans just weren't used to from a famous athlete. He was eloquent, charming, egotistical, poetic, creative, and influential. He was able to create stories and spoken-word poetry on the fly and would deliver it with flourish. He has all the Gates that point to those traits, as well as having the Channel 64-47, which is the Channel of Abstraction. This would likely enable him to receive "downloads" of information and create the words in a way that was either entertaining or threatening, depending on your perspective. His poems and speeches were called the precursors to both hip-hop and rap, verses that would come along in the '80s and '90s. His list of quotes is amazing, entertaining, but also thoughtful, empowering, and provocative. One list had his ten best quotes; another had twenty-one best quotes; a third had thirty. Even Entrepreneur Magazine had an article with his quotes by business topic. I couldn't even find a list with all his quotes, although I'm sure one will be compiled as a book in the years ahead.

Here are a few of them:

> *"I know where I'm going and I know the truth, and I don't have to be what you want me to be. I'm free to be what I want."*
>
> *"The word 'Islam' means 'peace.' The word 'Muslim' means 'one who surrenders to God.' But the press makes us seem like haters."*
>
> *"I hated every minute of training, but I said, 'Don't quit. Suffer now and live the rest of your life as a champion.'"*
>
> *"I am an ordinary man who worked hard to develop the talent I was given. I believed in myself, and I believe in the goodness of others."*

Read more at:

http://www.brainyquote.com/quotes/authors/m/muhammad_ali.html

"The Greatest" will be missed!

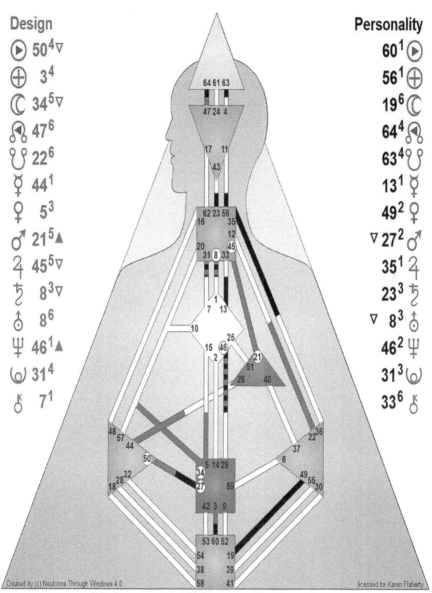

Design

- ⏵ $50^4\triangledown$
- ⊕ 3^4
- ☽ $34^5\triangledown$
- ☊ 47^6
- ☋ 22^6
- ☿ 44^1
- ♀ 5^3
- ♂ $21^5\blacktriangle$
- ♃ $45^5\triangledown$
- ♄ $8^3\triangledown$
- ⚷ 8^6
- ♆ $46^1\blacktriangle$
- ☋ 31^4
- ☌ 7^1

Personality

- 60^1 ⏵
- 56^1 ⊕
- 19^6 ☽
- 64^4 ☊
- 63^4 ☋
- 13^1 ☿
- 49^2 ♀
- $\triangledown 27^2$ ♂
- 35^1 ♃
- 23^3 ♄
- $\triangledown 8^3$ ⚷
- 46^2 ♆
- 31^3 ☋
- 33^6 ☌

Muhammad Ali Human Design chart

The great thing about the clarity exercise in this chapter—as you may have already figured out—is that you can use it for anything, not just your career. I actually had a chapter for abundance in my original outline, but opted to omit it, as it seemed redundant when we've already discussed this manifesting exercise. You can try this at home. Be my guest. It works.

And creating abundance of all sorts in your life brings us to the spirituality in your life. Abundance and spirituality go hand in hand. Whether you "believe" or not, don't skip this one. It plays a bigger role than you may think.

Chapter 6
Your Spirituality

Issues: Who am I? Why am I here? What's my purpose?

> "I know that I will infuriate a lot of people. But you know we're not born in sin; we're not here in this life to make good. The reality is that we come in innocent. We are innocent. We come into our journey, we come into our incarnation. It is not as if all of us can do God's will. It is not true. Some can consistently do God's will or anybody else's will. But others cannot."   Ra Uru Hu, 1999.

Let's take a look at spirituality, now that we've covered some of the really in-your-face issues that come up for all of us. If you're anything like me, that's taken a back seat for some time. Not intentionally. I knew it was always there, but more in the background. For a long time, it always seemed as if there were more important issues to handle. Little did I know how much ignoring this one would cost me.

After years and years of generally ignoring my physicality, my passions, my Inner Guidance, and my spirituality—even as I dutifully worked a lot, helped everyone who needed it, and went to church every Sunday—I realized that things were starting to break down. By my forties, I wasn't happy or fulfilled or fertile or even feeling particularly blessed. I was miserable in my job in New York City, commuting back and forth for twelve-hour days, without hobbies, no time to see friends or family, and unsuccessful in having children. Not a very optimistic time. It took a few more years to leave the job in the city, start feeling a little better with more conscious eating, sleeping, and exercise habits, and enough therapy to help me get past the depression of infertility. And then along came Human Design. What a godsend!

One of the things I love about Human Design: There is no pain or suffering in the Human Design chart. There is no procrastination; no racism; no sexism; no hatred; no gender. And every answer I've ever needed since I first got my chart in 2009 has been found somewhere in the chart.

And the bottom line spiritually becomes: We are all one. We have nothing to fear; it's all about the love.

I found this short article recently on Facebook and thought I'd share it. Now that I have my Human Design chart and all its answers, I no longer go to therapy sessions. I wish I had known about this before—it seems like a much simpler way to ask someone what's up with them when something's wrong. What do you think?

Dancing and Singing

"In many shamanic societies, if you came to a shaman or medicine person complaining of being disheartened, dispirited, or depressed, they would ask one of four questions.

When did you stop dancing?

When did you stop singing? When did you stop being enchanted by stories?

When did you stop finding comfort in the sweet territory of silence?

> Where we have stopped dancing, singing, being enchanted by stories, or finding comfort in silence is where we have experienced the loss of soul.
>
> Dancing, singing, storytelling, and silence are the four universal healing salves."
> **~ The Four-Fold Way: Walking the Paths of the Warrior, Healer, Teacher, and Visionary**
> From Project Happiness on Facebook, April 12, 2015

Doesn't that simplify things? And really, what is it that causes our suffering when it doesn't occur in our Human Design chart? If it's not Nature, then it must be Nurture, and how creative must we silly humans be to come up with all these detours in life??

Illusions and Our Suffering

There was an excerpt recently from a new book by Robert Wright called, *Why Buddhism is True: The Science and Philosophy of Meditation and Enlightenment.* Pretty heady title, and who knew that Buddhism had to be confirmed as true, after such a long stretch in history? The article explained simply what Buddhism was about—and this explanation was new to me. He describes it as a good news/bad news story.

We as humans are all prone to illusion—making things up that either make us feel better or make us feel worse. Usually—at least for many of us—the illusions don't make us feel very good. And often this leads to suffering of all sorts—worrying, regret, unhappiness, lack of fulfillment, and much more. But the good news, again according to Wright, is that illusions and suffering are one and the same, because we are the source of both, and if we could see the world clearly, then our suffering would stop. And therefore, we have the ability to stop the illusions **and** our suffering. Hence the song I've quoted from before: "We are our suffering."

Wright also notes that we're prone to illusion as a means of survival—almost as if Buddha and Darwin were partners in the science of evolution. Darwin probably would have approved of Buddha's solutions—like mindfulness, meditation, and gratitude—and Buddha would have probably appreciated Darwin's theories of evolution. Each would have seen the illusions for what they are—a means of survival in the days when we were hunter-gatherers. But most of us are not in that role anymore and certainly not in fear for our survival. And unfortunately for us now, the illusions we create usually lead to suffering in one form or another.

So what good do these illusions—the ones brought on by our fight or flight response—really do for us anymore? Do the illusions we create before a big event—whether it's a presentation to a large group, a date with a new person, sending our children off to a new school, or a confrontation with our boss—spur us on to success or to crumble in anxiety? We all have ways of dealing with these situations—hopefully in better ways as we mature—than we did the first time it happened. So we adapt. We adapt our feelings, our skills, our social behaviors, and maybe even our beliefs about the situation so that our lives improve and our anxieties decrease over time. That makes sense, right?

But what about those *other* illusions? The little ones we deal with almost every single day. The ones that cause the incessant chatter in our otherwise nimble brains. We can think of these as the "woulda, coulda, shoulda" illusions. The ones that show up at the most inopportune moments—partly because they are there to protect us...from the woolly mammoths of old! There is no logical reason for these fears, illusions, or worry. We know that logically we *can* do this (fill in the blank) activity! Usually, it's our gut that's saying "yes" while our head is screaming, "*Noooo!*" We don't need to get into all the ways this can happen—I'm sure you already recalled a few of them as you read this! But can you also recall that the majority of those situations turned out just fine? I read that over ninety-eight percent of the things we normally worry about *never* happen at all. All the boogie men in our heads, the nightmares in broad daylight, the horrible things we imagine might happen *never* happen at all!

So we could ask ourselves where these fears and illusions come from. And Robert Wright would say they're part of our evolutionary process. Well, that's nice, you might say, but what do I do today while waiting to evolve into a less anxious mortal??

Today, I'll suggest two tools. Of course, every challenge that I run across can use Human Design as a ready tool. You probably figured that. Knowing your own Human Design can help to dispel so many of the illusions that we face. When you know who you really are, a lot of illusions of who we think are, who we should be, who we're expected to be by parents, bosses, and spouses, go away. We stand in our truth and have the power to quiet the thoughts that used to rob us of our true identity and purpose.

The second tool, as Robert Wright suggests, is the age-old Buddhist practice of mindfulness meditation, which also works beautifully. It always has and probably always will. With a little practice and attention to your thoughts, feelings, and everything around you, it's a lovely way to decrease stress, find stillness, and allow for gratefulness to become a much more prominent part of your life. When you emerge from your stillness in meditation, the breath and the stillness can both be recalled and achieved at other stressful times of your day—if and when you take a moment to recall them. (I admit it—that's the hard part—remembering that there's a better way in the midst of stress!) But taking that breath and finding stillness—that allows for the real payoff: clarity in the present moment. Instead of anxiety, your head becomes clear, you can see the players and situation for what they really are, and then—with clarity—make a rational choice, a judicious comment, or offer a kind embrace. A "WTF" moment becomes a moment of calm, composure, and intuitive knowing-ness. You got this! And in the end, you make the world a better place.

Isn't that what we're all here for anyway?

Goal: Finding Inner Peace and Oneness

So if we're here to make the world a better place, to live in harmony with our communities, to help others, and to bring others joy, why is it so hard to find that inner peace and oneness for ourselves on a more consistent basis? I would suggest that it's our consciousness, and that if we were more "conscious" of it, we wouldn't bumble around for so long. So how can we do that?

Is Human Design the Science of Consciousness?

Have you heard of TED? I love watching the brilliant topics that TED brings to life for us as educational videos. These are amazing people who are experts in their fields putting their own spin on anything from the mundane to the absurd and everything in between! (www.TED.com) So when I recently saw a new release called, "How do you explain consciousness?" I was curious. David Chalmers, a philosopher at New York University, said, "There's nothing we know about more directly...but at the same time, it's the most mysterious phenomenon in the universe." So he shares some ways to think about the "movie playing in our heads."

He suggested that scientists don't know yet how to distinguish whether there is consciousness or not—or at least they don't agree on how to do that. Even talking about consciousness as a science, he said, was rather controversial in academia because "science" is considered to be purely objective while "consciousness" is considered to be subjective—that is, we each have one, but mine is different than yours! (It's sounding a lot like Human Design at this point. There is a video on YouTube as well as on the TED.com site, if you'd like to view it.)

Chalmers began with many reasons for why consciousness is hard to define. About halfway through his talk, he got to the heart of it. He posited two "crazy ideas" whose time had come, he thought at least, to be considered and that would help to define consciousness. The first idea was that it is "fundamental"—as fundamental a law in science as gravity, time, space, and energy. On that point, I would have to agree. What are we as humans or animals without a blip on the heart monitor or taking our first breath? Doesn't that define us—by defining the beginning of our life, and when it's gone, the end of our life? Even someone in a coma has consciousness—as they're happy to tell us once they're out! (See Simon Lewis's talk called, "Don't take Consciousness for Granted," at TED in December, 2010.)

David's second "crazy idea" is that consciousness is universal. Again, this totally makes sense to me and to Human Design. Human Design ascribes a chart to everything—humans, animals, plants, and even to inanimate objects like rocks and sand. We each are made up of atoms and, therefore, energy. We all vibrate—though at different rates, of course—and are part of life on the planet. So, we are all part of the global consciousness, too, while maintaining our own unique consciousness. All those individuals with consciousness become one large pulsing, vibrating mass on Planet Earth and we're all interconnected! How could we not be so, when a typhoon in Malaysia will cause a Polar Vortex in July in most of the US a week later? How could we not be inter-connected when the death of a young Middle Easterner or refugee children on the US border pulls on the heart strings of so many? Or when a royal wedding in the UK or the Winter Olympics are watched by billions of people in the same timeframe?

And yet we each have our own work to do, our own life to live, and our life's purpose to fulfill. Perhaps the dilemma comes for the scientists when they keep trying to lump us into groups, when in fact each of us is so unique as to defy any simple categorization. Even in Human Design, we start with five Energy Types, twelve Profiles and seven Authorities, but quickly move into so many different gates and channels that our uniqueness is completely evident once we know our Design! My geeky husband and I actually tried one day to figure out how many different Human Design combinations there might be on the planet and came up with 3.5 billion.

As Ra Uru Hu, the founder/creator of Human Design, explained so succinctly:

> "When you are looking at different activations in a chart, you are looking at the unique imprint of a person. We have receptors to everything. Everything that is white (on the chart) is a receptor. The imprint is what makes you different; it isn't what makes you the same. What makes us the same is the whole map in its entirety; what makes us different is our individual imprint. This is the Science of Differentiation, and Human Design teaches us about our uniqueness, what it is to be uniquely ourselves within the totality."
>
> *From "The Definitive Book of Human Design: The Science of Differentiation," p. 35.*

Ironically, Chalmers, at TED, started his talk on consciousness by saying that science is objective because it is repeatable. Having personally run thousands of Human Design charts, I and my Human Design colleagues can attest to the "repeatability" of Human Design, as well as its accuracy and uncanny ability to act as the "instruction manual" for one's life. So I guess it's only a matter of time before someone will be up on the stage at a TED conference, letting the world know about the new science of consciousness—Human Design. But for now, we can start by allowing Dr. Chalmers' "crazy ideas" into the lexicon or ponder them on a lazy summer afternoon!

Solutions:

Solutions for Peaceful and Consistent Spirituality in Your Life

Finding your own solutions to a spiritual practice that leads to inner peace and joy on a consistent basis may be as unique as your Human Design. I can't tell you exactly *what* to do on your path, but I can make some suggestions that have worked for me and my clients in terms of how to get back on the path.

The first thing I would suggest is grounding yourself or finding ways to center yourself. Most of us become so harried after a week of work, household chores, and family needs, that we think a short nap or reading for a half hour is enough to recharge us. That's rarely the case, especially if you're already burned out. And I get that you don't feel like you have the time to give to yourself. As if that's a selfish thing. I'll repeat what I said in the chapter on Health: No one can take care of you except you. It's not selfish; it's vital to your health and well-being. It's vital also to your spirituality. If you're not watching out for it, no one else will.

There are lots of ways to ground yourself—find a way that's most comfortable for you. Journaling, meditation, walking in nature, a yoga practice, and/or a Gratitude Journal, for example. Those are just a few ways—you or your friends may know of others. The more consistent you can be, the better. Even if it's just a few minutes every day to start, you can work yourself up to whatever works for you in terms of time you can spend versus what helps you to feel better and more grounded. Your practice will change over time, but so will you.

Finding Your Life's Purpose

Framework for Discovery - Parts of the Chart

We've talked quite a bit about Human Design in the book, but you probably won't be surprised to hear that there's more to take in and more parts of it that may help you to gain more awareness. Here's my complete framework for taking a client through the various parts of the Human Design chart. These pieces complete the picture of who you are and who you are here to be. It forms the acronym EMBRACE:

EMBRACE YOUR HUMAN DESIGN—BE WHO YOU'RE HERE TO BE

E: Energy Type and Strategy
M: Making decisions according to Strategy and Authority
B: Be who you are (your defined Energy Centers)
R: Raised with Conditioning (open centers) that leads to Wisdom
A: Alignment with Source/Law of Attraction
C: Chiron and Incarnation Cross as Life Purpose expression
E: Evolving into who you are here to be

When you find out more about your Human Design, either through other books, videos, or a complete Human Design session, you'll find out about your Incarnation Cross, your Chiron return, and other pieces that come together to make up the whole of you. Your Incarnation Cross is the story of your life *if* you are living out your Human Design Strategy and makes up about seventy percent of your personality traits. Your Chiron return tells us the theme of your life's purpose—just a theme, but the majority of my clients love the specificity of it and find that they truly resonate with it. And usually, it's something they realized a long time ago. So it's a relief in a way—like coming home to an old friend.

Trusting the Universe

The final piece to consistent spirituality is trusting the Universe. We've already talked about this, so I'll repeat it as a reminder. You can't move into your intentions without trust. Not trusting in the Universe is like giving your dinner order to the waiter at a fine restaurant and then knocking on the kitchen door to ask where it is again and again. What kind of behavior is that?

You'll feel so much happier, more aligned, and more purposeful when you can let go of all the past limiting beliefs and put your trust in the fact that we're all taken care of. We're here to be of service, yes, but the first part of the service is to *you*. If you can take care of your health, your purpose, and thus, your spirituality, you'll have inner peace and sleep like a baby each night.

Here's a profile of someone who lost her voice after a horrific event and then when she found her voice again, she kept going and going until her last day here.

Celebrity Profile: Maya Angelou

Maya Angelou
Splenic Manifestor
Born: Marguerite Johnson in Saint Louis, Missouri, on April 4,
1928, at 2:10pm
Died: Wednesday, May 28th, 2014, in Winston-Salem, NC, at the age
of 86
"There is no greater agony than bearing an untold story inside
you." – Maya Angelou, from her best-seller and award-winning
book, *I Know Why the Caged Bird Sings.*

Poet, author, speaker, activist, teacher, actress, dancer, singer, and
more! When you see a list of career titles like that, it tells you first
that it was a life well lived, but it also points to someone who's a
Manifestor. The more I read the obituaries for Maya Angelou when
she passed away in 2014, the more amazed I was with all the things
she had accomplished in her life. I knew of many of them, but the
more I read, the more titles there were to add. As a young woman,
she even worked as a streetcar operator in San Francisco and in a
brothel before she owned it!

If you've seen her on Oprah, or at the White House, or at Clinton's
inaugural, or on a stage somewhere, you've probably been
impressed with her diction, her amazingly deep and resonant voice,
her command of the language (she speaks a few), and her incredible
presence (she's six feet tall!). As one commentator proclaimed,
"Everything she said sounds like poetry!" She just has the kind of
voice that you can listen to while being inspired, motivated, or
calmed. She was truly a Renaissance woman in all of her actions and
words!

It was not surprising then to discover that she was a Manifestor
when I ran her chart. As a Manifestor, she did what she wanted to do

when she wanted to do it. After a childhood rape (at the age of seven), she stopped talking for six years after the conviction and subsequent murder of her attacker at the hands of her uncles. Very traumatic for a child, but such will, such tenacity, and being okay with who she was becoming are all signs of a young Manifestor finding her way in a segregated and hostile world during the Depression. It's a tale of courage that few children could have survived so spectacularly. So what was it about her chart that sparked her trajectory from obscurity in Arkansas to world renown?

First and foremost, it's Maya Angelou's Energy Type as the Manifestor, which gives her an extraordinary capacity to speak with people, bring them into her aura and then invite them to be a part of any activities she's decided to involve herself in. Of course, many of her activities were solo to an extent, but you probably know that you don't accomplish that much success without teams along the way. Whether it was her publishers, her acting coaches, her activist colleagues, which included Dr. Martin Luther King Jr. and Malcolm X, or her business partners, she was surrounded by people who could push her spirited works forward into the public realm.

Her Strategy as the Manifestor is to inform first, and while I didn't read any particular instance of her "*not informing*" the people who needed to know certain things, I got the feeling that she played her activities rather close to the vest and wasn't looking for others' opinions to make her own decisions. Her Authority was Splenic, which means that she would have an idea in her head, and then decide instinctively whether or not to act upon it. That kind of "knowing" plays well for a leader, a teacher, and an activist. She needn't consult anyone but herself when making any decision. It likely made her seem regal, assured, self-confident, and a little above it all. And she was.

The combination of gates and channels that she possessed added up to a queenly stature that she possessed from her late teens. Her channels (or themes of her life) included: the Money Line (always nice to have), the Channel of Talent—a combination of enthusiasm and depth, and the Channel of Initiation—a combination of Shock and the Love of Spirit. Rather simply, then, her ability to bring her students, fans, and audiences closer to the Love of Spirit via her various breadth of talents brought her substantial prosperity over the years.

Maya Angelou was such an icon throughout her life that her contributions will never be forgotten. Through her own initiation into Spirit, she was able to walk the bridge from tragedy to success with her words and her actions time and again as a teacher and mentor for many.

And of course, Maya Angelou had the Gate 56—the Storyteller. What a fitting legacy she's left as a storyteller!

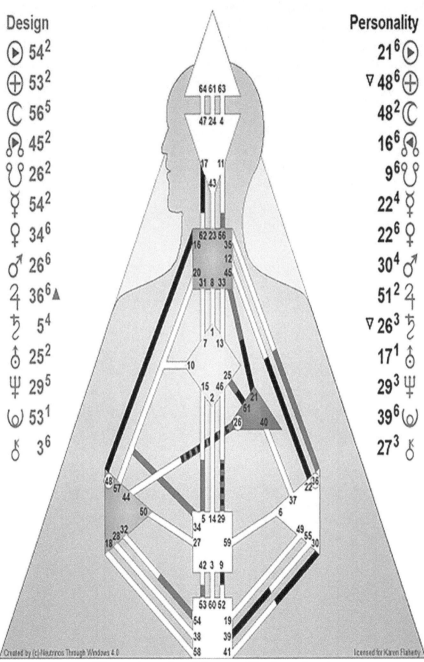

Maya Angelou Human Design chart

Why are we so afraid of reaching out to others, to be the voice we have within, to live our life's purpose to the fullest? No, we're not all Manifestors with the Channels of Talent and the Money Line to define us. But we do each have our own way of living out the fullest expression of our Human Design chart. It's not a secret anymore.

Chapter 7.

Next Steps on Your Path

The Human Design Principles in Action

It's been just over thirty years (January 1–8, 1987) since Human Design was first received by Ra Uru Hu in Ibiza, Spain!

As Human Design has evolved over this time, much has been written, interpreted, analyzed, and dissected about Human Design, its origins, and what it's supposed to do.

Do?

No, it's much more of a process! Human Design is here to help us understand ourselves. To understand others—our family, our friends, colleagues—in a way that empowers and encourages all of us.

It's like a long hug from an old friend. It feels good, it feels right, like we've known it all along and wish it would never end. We just had to be reminded.

And what are we reminded of?

We're reminded of our brilliance, our genius, our very unique reason for being here, our traits and our skills, our talents and preferences, our energy blueprint—and how it differs from others— our decision-making Strategy and lots more. Your Human Design chart contains specific, accurate, and reliable information. The kind of information—in the form of accolades, compliments, confirmations of our goodness—that we were happy to hear from our grandparents or favorite aunt or uncle or teacher when we were growing up.

"Oh, you're so _____ (fill in the blank with your favorite childhood trait)."

They knew that trait was real and blossoming in you because they knew you. They watched you with an unconditional love that may have been infrequent, maybe even rare, during your childhood. But in you, they could see glimpses of genius, apparitions of the future you, flickers of the real you shining through. They not only saw those flickers, they appreciated them and encouraged them. Those dear family members or teachers were aware of the authentic you—perhaps even before you were aware of how special you are.

Fast forward thirty, forty, or fifty years…

So what now? Now that you *are aware* of how truly special you are or are about to be? Now that you're living (or are about to live) your authentic life, knowing exactly who you are and what you're here for, guess what? It's Show Time!

(And if you're **not** feeling particularly authentic yet, isn't it time to get right with that part of you? A not-so-subtle hint: A Human Design session or coaching session can help you do exactly that.)

On the other hand, if you've found your way to this book and have read this far, then I have a special message for you as we finish up. I thank you for your persistence in finding out more, but also ask that you keep your purpose in mind as you read this last chapter.

Yes, it's Show Time! The world is evolving, energies are shifting—you can feel the whoosh, can't you? Many people are already living their "Heaven on Earth." Now is the time for you to help or assist or cajole the rest of the planet into the reality of a peaceful, nurturing, and sustainable planet.

You, as Lightworkers, are needed to help in this process. I'm not saying it will necessarily be easy, but it is what we're here for. This incarnation—right now—is a time for us to get on our path, do the work that fulfills us best, and help the people who are just awakening to the possibilities that you've been aware of—even if that's a relatively short time! We only have to be a few steps ahead of our brothers and sisters to help them to awaken, give them a hand up, lend some guidance at the right time, and make a huge difference in their lives.

If you know why you're here and know what makes you happy, fulfilled, and content, then this is your time to step out. Baby steps are fine. Actually, they're the best way to step onto your path. (If you take a scary, big step instead, any negative effects might cause you to withdraw back into your shell—and not come out till it feels safe again. And you might miss the Show!)

So take some baby steps to get you started, you'll gain momentum as you go, and trust that you're strong enough—plenty strong enough—to do this. It's what you're here for, you're perfect for the "job," and no one else can do your role but *you*!

So give yourself a high-five in the mirror, get excited about the adventure of it, decide with clarity what your first step will be, and let's roll. It's Show Time on Planet Earth!

Exactly how can you get to feel like it's Show Time if you're still thinking in terms of right and wrong, good and bad, black and white, up and down??

Duality vs. Oneness

Are we ready for oneness? Are we ready to give up the pretense of duality and come together as one people on this beautiful Earth so that we're working together, playing together, breathing together, joyful together? Is it time?
We may not be completely ready just yet, but it feels like we're on the cusp of great movement. It feels like we've made significant

progress just in the past few months. Once again, we've had violence in the US, Europe, and the Middle East, disruption of the world economy with Britain's exit from the EU, a new female prime minister in Great Britain, and some critical weather patterns. The stark contrast between what's visible and apparent vs. what we want—or say that we want—is reaching epic levels. A shift is occurring.

How can we say we want peace and love and yet be confronted each day—whether you experience it first-hand or via social media and TV—with the opposite??

Remember the story I told in the first chapter? About my Aunt Mary and the Summer of 1967? It was the "Summer of Love" for many, but for me it was a summer of awakening to the violence, racism, and hatred in the world. My little dysfunctional cocoon burst and would never go back to the way it was. I'm sure I'm not the only one who was feeling that way fifty years ago, a few times in between or always, and is now feeling it again with a new set of circumstances.

I saw a video on Facebook recently of a black man, surrounded by his white wife and their children, asking via poster board why we see the contrast as black vs. white when it's really about dark vs. light? In his video, the dark is about hate and fear; the light is about love. While our confrontations are showing up as racial divides, there is fear on both sides, and it's the fear that causes turmoil.

This is the time for the fears to be replaced with discussion, understanding, grace under pressure, and eventually peace and love. At least that's what I'm hoping for.

As President Obama said in Dallas at the memorial service for the slain police officers in 2016, "Can we find the character, as Americans, to open our hearts to each other?"
I hope so. I pray so. I intend and imagine and envision so.
Beyond believing that we are all One, it really helps to be grateful most of the time. Whether you use a Gratitude Journal or some other

way to keep the gratitude flowing daily, it's important now to make it a priority and intend that the future will be bright for you and your family and the entire planet.

LOVE and LOSS—and Gratitude

In November of 2014, my parents would have celebrated their sixtieth anniversary. They got married the weekend before Thanksgiving in 1954 in Newark, NJ, at the now-demolished, but grand in its time, Military Park Hotel. Friends and relatives always talked fondly of that wedding. It was a beautiful affair, they all said. They both lived a full life with six children, many friends and family around, and lots of happy memories, especially toward the end of their lives, when they retired to Florida and had a little honeymoon again—just the two of them. Lots of visits from the kids and grandkids, of course, but it gave them a kind of peace that's good for the soul and rekindled their love for life and for each other. We loved those visits!

My parents have both passed now. My father passed in 2003 on their forty-ninth anniversary—with a wonderful priest doing a wedding vow renewal and last rites at the same time—and my mother passed in 2009, just a week after my brother died suddenly; the stress was too much for her heart. She said that she didn't want to go to his wake—and she didn't!

I mention this because each November it's still a little sad, and yet we all go through loss in our lives. Not many of us get to be middle-aged, or even younger, without experiencing the loss of someone who is close to us—whether it's a grandparent or parent, a favorite aunt or uncle, or a friend's "early" death. So when we have a family event, we can gather with friends and family and remember the ones who have passed on, too. They're probably all around the table enjoying the celebration anyway!

That's my belief! I like having them around!
Mike Dooley, the author of many books and creator of "Notes from the Universe" at www.tut.com, came out with a book not too long

ago called *The Top Ten Things that Dead People Want to Tell You*. I haven't read the whole book yet, but the premise is that while we may pass away from this lifetime, our souls live on. And they live on pretty happily, thank you very much, he writes!

Things are pretty good on the other side, Mike proclaims, and the souls are having quite a celebration for all they accomplished on Earth, a reunion with friends and family, and feelings of relief all around. But mostly it's all about love. In the absence of pain, fear, illness, petty fighting, betrayal and angst, all that's left is love. They're kind of bathed in it. For those of us left behind, that can be a happy thought. No matter what the circumstances of the death are, the soul goes on and lives on in a love-filled environment that makes any happy moments down here pale in comparison. That helps me to feel better about any loss. How about you?

What I found most reassuring about the book were these three ideas: they were ready to leave, we're *not* ready, and there are no mistakes. Whoa! That's a whole lot of matter-of-fact, in-your-face common sense all at once!

Of course, I've heard each of these ideas before, but when they're in one place, it kind of hits you over the head. Kind of a slap-your-forehead moment! What am I worrying about, or more precisely, why am I worrying about them? They're fine and they want us to move on. Move on with life, move on with those around us who are living, and move on with love. There's so much to do in the present moment, and it's so easy so ensconce ourselves in memories, sorrow, grief, and even depression over a loved one's passing. But "in reality," they want us to go on living and just remember the happy memories and use them as lessons.

And why not?

Usually their life and their death left us with valuable lessons, didn't they? Even if they left early, that was a lesson to their peers to drive safely or lose weight or get a little more exercise or treat the connections that are most meaningful to us as if they are. If they left after a full life, there were likely lots of lessons, too, if we look closely. In retrospect, it's usually easy to see that they got what they gave, and their wisdom shone through all their actions—whether they were big or small. It's a lesson to live in the present moment, put down our cell phones sometimes, and just breathe the cool, fresh air of the season, or play with the kids, or call a parent. While we still can.

No regrets for past mix-ups or missed opportunities, no guilt or blame required—just do it now.

Have a good time with the little ones, and the big kids, and the family we haven't seen for a while! Relish the gratefulness of it all. I'm grateful especially for our health, for the wonderful life we've created in our new place, for our friends and family and their continued health, for the beautiful views and nature that we enjoy each day, for the wonderful people I've met at the fairs and events over the past few years, for all the new people I'll be meeting, and for the wonder of this life, as it continues to unfold in often surprising and exciting ways!

Telling the World

Make America Kind...Again?

Thank you...to that twenty-five percent of the population—forty-seven percent of the electorate—who voted for Donald Trump as our forty-fifth president of the United States. You believed as you voted that we needed a change, a wake-up call, that the status quo wouldn't really work for us anymore. And you were right. I think we are ready for a change, too. But I was still surprised by the election's outcome. And I wondered...

I accept the election results now. The country and the world are changing. Our vibration is rising and the energy is moving much more quickly than before. Over the next decade, we'll be creating a new world, from what I can tell. We'll all be moving toward prosperity, vibrant health, peace in all corners of the world, and social justice. These goals will be the result of the majority of us acting out of empathy, kindness, goodness, and compassionate hearts. It could happen quickly, but as with all things of a human nature, we won't really *want* to change until we have to—until it's too painful not to change. That's part of the reason that the 2016 election in the US—and really all the elections around the world, such as Brexit—have been so abruptly divided with no middle ground. Half the world is ready to change and the other half isn't. On the tails of the election, we've experienced more divisive challenges with the #MeToo movement, gun violence, and racism.

A New Story

Maybe it's time we create a new story for our world. This is a quote from Charles Eisenstein in his essay, "Hate, Grief and a New Story," published right after the 2016 election:

> *"We are entering a space between stories. After various retrograde versions of a new story rise and fall and we enter a period of true unknowing, an authentic next story will emerge. What would it take for it to embody love, compassion, and inter-being? I see its lineaments in those marginal structures and practices that we call holistic, alternative, regenerative, and restorative. All of them source from empathy, the result of the compassionate inquiry: What is it like to be you?"*

Until we do collectively make the change to compassion, buckle your seat belts! It's going to be a bumpy ride! The changes may be turbulent, violent, and economically uncomfortable for some people. (For others, they will continue to create their worlds, living by their own intentions and enjoying their own version of Heaven on Earth!) Therefore, no matter who you voted for, it seems like there's a lot for us to do. Ready or not, the changes will be coming. So here's my personal to-do list to stay in kindness and empathy for the next few years:

Keep Learning. Know your craft, but learn something new, too. Keep up with technology (so your family doesn't think you're "old"). Learn more about whatever your passions are—hobbies, sports, travel. It's all good to know and keeps us sharp (vs. hiding out with TV binge-watching—not so much).

Know the Facts. Stay informed and know what's going on in the world from a variety of news sources. Social media, of course (be careful of the "fake" news stories), but sample others like network news, cable news, magazines. Talk to other people. They have "facts," too. But then do some research if you have more questions. One person suggested reading the actual newspaper—in print or online. For many, that's a novel idea. For those of us who still like reading the papers, it's reassuring! (Maybe we're not so old!)

Here's another quote from the Eisenstein essay—he understands that the rift in the country is from pain, all kinds:

"We've got to stop acting out hate. I see no less of it in the liberal media than I do in the right-wing. It is just better disguised, hiding beneath pseudo-psychological epithets and dehumanizing ideological labels. Exercising it, we create more of it. What is beneath the hate? My acupuncturist Sarah Fields wrote to me, 'Hate is just a bodyguard for grief. When people lose the hate, they are forced to deal with the pain beneath.'

"I think the pain beneath is fundamentally the same pain that animates misogyny and racism—hate in a different form. Please stop thinking you are better than these people! We are all victims of the same world-dominating machine, suffering different mutations of the same wound of separation. Something hurts in there. We live in a civilization that has robbed nearly all of us of deep community, intimate connection with nature, unconditional love, freedom to explore the kingdom of childhood, and so much more. The acute trauma endured by the incarcerated, the abused, the raped, the trafficked, the starved, the murdered, and the dispossessed does not exempt the perpetrators. They feel it in mirror image, adding damage to their souls atop the damage that compels them to violence. Thus it is that suicide is the leading cause of death in the U.S. military. Thus it is that addiction is rampant among the police. Thus it is that depression is epidemic in the upper middle class. We are all in this together.

"Something hurts in there. Can you feel it? We are all in this together. One earth, one tribe, one people."
Source: http://charleseisenstein.com/hategriefandanewstory

Stand up for what you believe in. Keep active with local charities, local politics, the School Board, and social causes. The 2016 election was won at the local, grass roots level—but not by the party that thought they had a wonderful ground game. Assumptions around voter identity politics shouldn't be taken for granted. We're all different and we've all got an opinion about what needs to be done. So speak up. If we start talking to each other, we'll come to compassion together and eventually reach consensus together. Hallelujah! Won't that be grand?

Be Kind. To everyone. We may not agree, but no one is less than you. All people deserve our respect. This is our classroom. Here's a song called "HumanKind" from Po A Tree, that I heard in yoga class one day: "We are all learning how to be HumanKind, so be kind." How true. Here are some of the lyrics:

"We're all learning how to be
Living breathing human beings
In a world full of others living too!
We're all dancing in a spiral
Even if we think we're falling down for a while
The only place to go from the bottom is up
So look at your cup

Cause I think it's full
This very lifetime is our school
And we're all learning how to be
HumanKind, So be kind."
HumanKind Lyrics from the Album "Sound of my Mother" by Po A
Tree
Source: "Sound of my Mother "full length album, released July 1, 2010

Have fun. Stay centered, stay focused on what you want to create, stay grounded. Do what feels good to you. The Law of Attraction works no matter who's in the White House, I promise you!

Whenever you're with family and friends, keep it friendly, but ask some of the questions you've been wanting to ask from a compassionate viewpoint. I have a feeling we'll all learn something about them *and* about ourselves!

This is what "A New Story" can look like—one that John's bio now tells, after discovering Human Design, peppered with a lot of resistance and much practice:

> "John knew from an early age that he would be doing something important in his life. He had no idea what that would be, but he knew it wouldn't be in his native Ireland. He was bound for the United States, in his mind, as soon as he heard his aunt talk about her anticipated journey when he was only four years old. He just couldn't convince his mother that the timing was right for them! So he waited, and finally at twenty-five years old, he made the trip with his brother and hasn't looked back.

> "As a master carpenter, John was a popular and impassioned employee, then manager, then partner in a number of carpentry and construction endeavors. But he always had that nagging feeling that he was supposed to be doing something to help people, and more than just

with their material wants. He started looking into books, courses, and seminars that would help him to discover his real purpose in this life. His studies led him to his own spiritual journey, which soon became a consuming hobby. Within a few years, he was studying with well-known healers and psychics, who encouraged him in his training, noting that his gifts were quite rare and would enable him to help many.

"John is now a healer, psychic, medium, and most of all, he's a compassionate listener. He'll have insights into any situation or circumstance that you present to him. He'll hear your questions, find your pain, connect with your Spirit, and complete your sentences by the end of a session. The gifts that John has used for years to interpret beautiful woods as a medium for artistry are now being used to interpret his clients' feeling, attitudes, and needs, to reassure, assist, and calm them so that their burdens are relieved."

Frankly, this is the kind of spiritual transformation that keeps me going, pushes me forward each day, and helps me to believe that the world would be a much kinder, safer, and more contented place if we all knew a little bit about Human Design.

Final Thoughts on how Human Design can Help

Our Shifting Consciousness

With all that's happening in the news and around the world, I've been feeling the energies shifting quite a bit since the New Year. Maybe you have, too?

As I tell my clients, the energies have definitely been shifting. What this feels like is a number of physical symptoms like: fatigue, interrupted sleep, joint pains, sensitivities to certain foods, headaches, and others.

Slowly but surely, the veil is lifting as we move into a new consciousness. The veil between us and other dimensions is becoming lighter and thinner; it allows us to see more clearly what's really going on all around us; it allows us to see the inconsistencies, the lies, the deceptions, and the inauthenticity.

It's not about conspiracy theories, although I've heard that explanation out there. What this is is a shifting of our consciousness that allows us to awaken to what's important to us and to our family and friends. As Ra used to say, it's time to stop being sheep, following the herd mentality. It's time to reclaim our power, live our decision-making Strategy, and find what truly makes us happy... and then do it.

The consciousness is changing and we can now take personal responsibility for each of our actions. We can take better care of ourselves so that we can thrive and so that we can do what we're really here to do. We can take care of our neighbors, family, and friends. But not in a "savior" way, the way we used to. That no longer works. We don't have to be martyrs or saints anymore for anyone else's sake. We can help others to help themselves—without fear, without lack. Let go of things that don't reflect our oneness.

The separation from Oneness is apparent in the news we hear too often, but then there's a silver lining. Too many industries to mention are having their deceptions revealed—and it's leading to increased transparency within corporations. Mass shootings are leading to outpourings of love and caring and true empathy that seem disproportionately larger than they would have been only a year ago. CEOs are leaving their positions in disgrace when their deceptive practices are revealed, and are replaced by younger, more diverse talent. Communities within our communities—like LGBTQ, and Muslims, and #MeToo or #TimesUp—are being embraced in unity for their contributions and values, because we are all in this together.

Political candidates are being vetted and either embraced or discarded based on their thinking: Are they moving forward into the new consciousness or not? That they present such a stark contrast this midterm election year is no accident. We needed to see such a contrast in order to pay attention at all. This is not a time for complacency or sitting on the sidelines. It's a time for active involvement.

All these inconsistencies are being shown to us so that we can make our own decisions.

Do you want a scarcity mindset or abundance?

Do you prefer authenticity from your leaders and CEOs or more deception?

Does corporate greed advance our world—or is a generous spirit more likely to help?
Do we benefit by all the little kindnesses we can offer each other on a daily basis or from the pettiness that we see on social media?

Are you ready to see more humans move away from chronic disease and embrace vibrant health?
Does it feel better to tacitly ignore the pollution we create daily or raise our heads up to see what we can do to help preserve Mother Earth for the coming generations?

Is it easier to carry around the fears and resentment and anger of years past, elections past, traumas past or to let go of those old wounds and create a new paradigm?

Is it time? Do you feel more urgency than you did a few years ago? Are you awakening to the truth? I am.

There is little separation anymore between us and Divine Love. With any thought we have, we are either adding to the Light of the world, or to the negativity of it. So the question is: How can I add to the Light of the world to create a Heaven on Earth?

I see more evidence of joy, unity, acceptance, love, and forgiveness each day. It's there. Just look for it. And then step into it in whatever way you can. It feels so much better!

#loveisloveisloveisloveisloveisloveislove…

I hope so. I pray so. I intend and imagine and envision so.

THANK YOU AND MAY I ASK A FAVOR??

Thank you so much for reading this book!! Did you enjoy it?

If you did, may I ask a favor of you?

Would you mind turning the page to write a review or go back to the book's Amazon page at this link:
https://www.amazon.com/dp/B07HB8PRHK

And leave a review with your opinion, perspectives, a-ha moments, or what you'd like others to watch for in the book as they read it!

Your review helps to spread the word about Human Design and how it can help people just like you to achieve joy in their lives!

And since that's my purpose too, I sincerely appreciate your help!

Testimonials

I am so blessed to have attracted some of the most wonderful, loving, and appreciative clients on the planet to my Human Design practice. Every day, they allow me to learn more about them and about myself so that I can help the next client with more wisdom, more genuine guidance, and more love. It is truly an honor to serve in this way. I thought you might like to hear some of their stories and results from having learned about their Human Design with me:

Good Morning all, I would like to share an amazing experience I had last night. I had a Human Design reading with Karen. I could not believe how accurate the reading was about how I work (so to speak). Karen went over my chart in great depth to help me understand myself.

I can't recommend Karen enough, she was thorough, patient, a wealth of knowledge, and ensured you understood your unique blueprint. She is an amazing and kind soul. I believe everyone should have a Human Design reading to help fully understand yourself, it's all there. In your own unique blueprint, your strengths, weaknesses, patterns, thoughts. It was a truly amazing gift to one's self, and I highly recommend Karen. She truly understands her craft and ensures she takes extreme care in explaining your Human Design.
  ■ Jennifer P., Chicago, IL

*

Thank you so much for last night. I'm still blown away! I feel so good today, a huge sense of relief and a massive pressure I've released from myself. I can say I'm starting to feel more like myself (I know sounds so silly, but I know you understand.) and trusting that and releasing the doubts I held around aspects of myself.

So many people's projections of me can just bugger off now! haha. Still a lot to work on but I feel so positive with the awareness I now have and what more I will develop to absolutely improve the quality of my life. YAY!! Thank you so much for what you do and allowing us to find confidence in exactly who we are. You are amazing!! I thoroughly enjoyed listening and talking with you last night, it was so much fun and will change my life forever. I certainly had a lot of a-ha moments, sooooo good!!!!

Thank you also for sending through the attachments and the audio recording (and follow-up checking I received them, you are wonderful!). I'm going to print them off now and jump into bed and read them. I will most definitely be recommending this to my friends and family!

It was privilege to have you helping me to have a better understanding myself and Strategy to live a fulfilling life. Very appreciated your generosity and professional services.

I'll listen to your recording and try to implement the strategies into my daily life
- Michelle H., Sydney, Australia

*

Karen did a Human Design reading for me that I thought was exceptional. Honestly, I felt like I was discussing my Human Design chart with a longtime friend. She was easy to talk to and went to great pains to discuss every aspect in detail to make sure that I understood what everything meant. And, as an added bonus, she even gave me some insight into both my husband's and daughter's charts. I am still blown away by how accurately Human Design defines me. So many things rang so true, and I learned things about myself that I suspected but didn't know were essentially a part of my DNA. I have also learned ways to live that will help me function to a higher degree. I highly recommend Karen if you want a reading. I can't think of anything she could have done better, particularly as she told me that if any questions came up that she would be more than happy to answer them.
- Victoria L., Savannah, GA

*

I had an illuminating Human Design reading with Karen. For the past five months, Karen has also been my Human Design coach. Our monthly sessions have helped me integrate what I learned about myself from my Human Design reading. Karen truly cares about how I am doing with my decision-making Strategy and gives me sage advice and support as I embark on my new career. It's a great pleasure to work with Karen, whose passion for Human Design shines through in every conversation we have.

■ Allison C., New York City

*

Thank you once again for the wonderful and profound experience. You are absolutely right about the a-ha moments...and there were more than a few. I'm already having fun following my Strategy and getting rid of old habits that I'd been conditioned with.

● Andre I., New York

*

Our talk gave me a lot to reflect on, and I look forward to seeing what changes I experience once I integrate the lessons I learn. The biggest difference I've noticed so far is the recognition of other people's energy. I'm still not sure on how to handle it, but I definitely am starting to feel a difference. I look forward to hearing from you, and thanks again for all of your help!

■ Christopher R., intuitive healing coach, NJ

*

Wow, Karen! Thank you very much for these recordings and the attachments! I have so thoroughly enjoyed this reading, and I am excited to make decisions according to my Strategy and Inner Authority. Speaking of Inner Authority, I'm so glad you included those questions for the Sacral response. I audibly responded with an upward/excited "mmm!" or "mm-hmm" for a yes and "meh" or a downward/indifferent "mmm" for a no.

It's so funny to me that you mentioned that knowing my true voice is part of the healthy state for the Throat center. The name of my voice class was "Awakening Your True Voice." It was spiritual in nature, and we happened to focus on proper breathing, being receptive to the music, and using our entire body as an instrument. When I told my friends about what I was learning, they would tell me, "That doesn't sound like a typical voice class! It sounds perfect for you." Granted, they are healers and artists, too, but still. :)

Monday's small-group voice class was fabulous. I used my gut to pick out the right place to sit, and the spot closest to the piano was perfect for me. After class, I had the chance to talk to my teacher, and I started talking to her about Human Design. She hadn't heard of it, but I at least planted the seed if it comes up again for her. Her teaching makes sense to me because she emphasized the Sacral as a Motor and to sing on impulse (i.e., sense the music in your external reality and wait to respond to the music when it feels right).

Oh, and thank you so much for making the comment that combining singing with healing would be interesting to you. It's actually what I want to do! Whenever I sing, I set the intention to activate healing energy and can feel the energy in my Throat. One of the healing modalities I work with, the Aka Dua, is a very creative, healing energy. I've done some experiments with some of my energetically sensitive healer friends, and they can feel that energy in my recordings. It's really cool!
- Allison C., singer, New York

*

Thank you so much, Karen. I must confess I had my doubts about Human Design before our session, but I truly enjoyed it, and it has given me a tremendous boost to have more confidence and insight in my endeavors in the days and weeks ahead.
- Lois F., Morristown, NJ

*

"Those who know me know I am a big believer in energy, intuition, and destiny, etc. So I was thrilled when I met Karen, received my chart, and even more so when she did my reading.

This was such a powerful and comforting call that gave me so much clarity, quite a bit of a-ha moments as well as those "ah, that explains it" ones... But most of all, it uncovered and verbalized quite a few things I have been feeling in regards to my business that I was unable to pinpoint until yesterday.

I am convinced that everybody should get their reading to get a better understanding of themselves, so they can live a more meaningful, peaceful, and purposeful life.

Thank you, Karen!

- Sara S., social media coach, New York

*

TANGIBLE RESULTS

I loved working with Karen, she held my hand with her sensitivity to my unique personality.

She allowed me to explore my vision and talents as a Projector (5/1). I gained a better understanding of how I move forward in the world, particularly knowing being asked, being invited, as an opportunity. Once I let that invitation come in, I can really enjoy it; once people tune into me they get me, so being more spiritual and soft is powerful.

I also realized I am a wise seductive energy, I am quiet, and people will understand me and ask me more advice if I move from that place. This information has transformed me if I stay focused on it. I don't have to be a loud person to be received.

Learn to operate in my Law of Attraction. Manifesting invitation, which is so powerful!

Believe in myself. What I need to realize to focus on it more monthly, weekly to make it aligned.

OTHER TRANSFORMATIONS

Being more aware of my Projector, reminding myself that I don't have sustainable energy, and taking in too much energy in from people can affect me.

Using my energy in a wise way...

This has been validating information for me, that I have to honor my self-care.

Importantly, the invitation aspect is valuable so I don't throw myself on people.

This is a good roadmap since I am twenty percent of the people, and most of my life I can't sustain myself.
I was invited to use my storytelling in different mediums, Karen was a good guide to tune into
my creativity and operate my business that works by people coming toward me.

A work in progress.

WHAT IT WOULD HAVE COST ME NOT DOING THE CHART

I think if I didn't do the reading, I might have not been as effective in achieving success and results out in the world of my true intuitive talents. It gave me a better insight and understanding on how I am perceived and what works for me as a sensitive person and wait for my waves that's best for me.
I like the peace, wait to be asked for an answer rather than offer it before the question is asked upon me. This helped me save a lot of unwanted energy in social situations and gave me a tremendous amount of confidence and strength around people.
I have to remember to do this and use it in my business.

WHAT ARE THE BIGGEST SOURCE OF PAIN

I am not sure if I came in with a lot of pain, but rather confusion of my purpose.
Why I am not being received, so this affirms if I operate on my unique energy, people will find me. This is HUGE!

This helped me learn how to be more fluid in the world and protect my energy in a quiet, spiritual way, and people will find me.

I have confidence issues, so to have validation of my creative and source energy supports me and my business by being an intuitive leader. I learned not force my energy, so this helps me by being more mindful of my natural tendency and let the big positive energy come toward me and visualize what I want, as an imaginative person, very useful.

Be more refined...Thank you so much Karen, I almost feel every year I need to be reminded of my powerful parts of my chart.
- Jane M., Photographer/lifestyle coach, New Jersey

*

What specific (tangible, if appropriate) results did you get from having a Human Design reading with me?

1.***I have a better understanding about my children's HD and how to communicate with them. This makes all of us happier and better connected.
*** I have learned to accept what the universe shows me.
*** I have learned to trust and not negatively react.
*** resiliency to life

2. What other transformations happened in your life because of these results?

*** great relationship with my kids, ex, friends, parents
***great job
***utilizing forgiveness
***accepting who I am
***I understand me and my emotional wave—I see life as is and understand my HD and how to use it to make better decisions.
***I see and follow my inner feelings and gut—I wait to respond

3. What do you imagine would have been the cost to you had you NOT decided to have a Human Design reading?
***I would have stayed stuck in anger after divorce and unemployment. I would not be as connected and close to my kids, as I was yelling and controlling them too much before learning about their HD.

4.   What were the biggest sources of pain, if any, that you were eager to solve when you decided to have the reading with me?
*** relationships, parenting, handling changes, emotional wave reactions
 • Andrea D., salesperson/mother, CT

*

Thank you so much for your request! I'd be honored to answer the questions and give you some insight into the incredible, life-changing way Living by Human Design has affected my world.

1. What specific (tangible, if appropriate) results did you get from having a Human Design reading with me?

a. My job. My design and reading pointed to the fact that it takes a while for me to acclimate to a job. This can involve pain in the beginning (I tend to be a perfectionist). Not wanting to experience pain at this point in my life and realizing I have a great deal of influence in my current occupation, I made the decision to stay in Jacksonville and remain in the same job I am currently in. This has led to an incredible calm and sureness.
b. Location, location, location. I made a decision to move to the beach. The decision manifested into a tangible home one block from the Atlantic Ocean. I reside in Atlantic Beach. It is a miracle and still amazes me every day!

2. What other transformations happened in your life because of these results?

I think those two are the biggest realities. I believe my Strategy of "wait to respond" has given me pause on occasion. Looking for confirmation is now my new mantra.

Oh—and because I am a Generator—I am following the lead of those with the big ideas. I am the get-it-done person. I add my creativity and the world expands for all of us! It's been a fun ride!

3. What do you imagine would have been the cost to you had you NOT decided to have a Human Design reading?

Pain. Isolation from my true self. I would have continued to try and 'force' all of my life choices, instead of waiting. Everything flows now.

4. What were the biggest sources of pain, if any, that you were eager to solve when you decided to have the reading with me?

Relationship direction. For now, that still has not been settled. I know that someone with their Throat Energy Center (filled? complete?) is the best match for me. I know who I am walking into a room. I am my work, sexual Sacral Center filled and full of confidence. For now, I am waiting to respond, I know a relationship will manifest in the proper time. :-)

Thank you! I have much more and would welcome a phone call to discuss, should this interest you. You are so GOOD.
- Elizabeth P., Florida

RESOURCES

Here are a few links to some of the places I turn to frequently to get energetic information from about how the planet and all its inhabitants are changing. I think you might like some of them, too.

www.espavo.org Steve Rother runs this site (formerly known as Lightworker.com) and channels. On the last Saturday of each month, they do free streaming of their 2-hour show. The first and last half hour is a live channel from "The Group." Lots of free videos, webinars, and articles on the website and on YouTube, as well as other classes and webinars that are fee-based.

www.eraofpeace.org Patricia Cota-Robles is one person I've seen live at seminars, and she channels a lot about how we're moving from 3D to 5D. She also talks a lot about God and how we got to this point with lots of Biblical touch-points, both Old and New Testament.

www.SpiritLibrary.org A whole group of curated authors, speakers, channels, etc., who submit their articles and videos here. Good place to find the most appealing teachers for you at this time!

https://www.abraham-hicks.com/This is the place that I was first introduced to information about the Law of Attraction. We didn't discuss this particular teacher, but if you haven't seen their work, it's key to a lot of the energetic changes going on right now and also works beautifully with Human Design. They have lots of free videos and articles on their site. They also do seminars all around the US.

https://tut.com Mike Dooley created this site about 20 years ago, and I've been getting his "Notes from the Universe" each weekday for almost that long. He writes and sends notes about how our "Thoughts become things" (his term for the Law of Attraction) that are encouraging, uplifting and always seem to touch the right chord. He also has a number of books and videos and does seminars around the world.

In addition, if you're interested in learning more about Human Design or in using it in your coaching practice, you can check out these three schools of Human Design which are geared to teachers, coaches and the curious ones!

Karen Curry Parker at The Quantum Alignment System

The International Human Design School
at https://www.ihdschool.com/

Chetan Parkyn & Carola Eastwood at Human Design for All
https://humandesignforusall.com

My thanks go out to each of these spiritual warriors, authors, and public figures who have been on the leading-edge of consciousness for so long.

ABOUT THE AUTHOR

Karen Flaherty brings many years of corporate business and life experience to her Human Design coaching practice. A graduate of the University of Pennsylvania in Philadelphia, Karen has worked in New York and New Jersey in marketing and sales positions. She's worked in the fields of sports licensing and merchandising, retailing, management consulting for the healthcare industry, and for the last ten years in Corporate Life, in the creation and sale of online training courses for corporations. In each position, she was fortunate to be working for the companies as they grew and prospered exponentially. This combination of experiences ignited a desire to help others in their challenges, especially with regard to self-awareness and stress management.

Soon after discovering Human Design, Karen realized this may be a way to follow a different path that also satisfied her yearning to make a difference and follow her life's purpose of empowering others to find their unique reason for being here. Karen has studied Human Design since 2009 and became a certified Human Design Specialist in 2010 through Karen Curry Parker. Since then, she has done dozens of holistic shows along the East Coast, running thousands of charts, and working with hundreds of clients, as she satisfied her very logical self that Human Design is the best way to allow people who are curious to discover their purpose and their unique genius.

After spending more than 35 years in Corporate America in those sales and marketing positions, Karen is happy now to be helping individuals, partners of all kinds, entrepreneurs, coaches, families, small business owners, and corporate managers find a new way of doing life and business in the 21st Century.

Karen enjoys doing her Human Design practice full time since moving to a small eclectic Florida beach town in 2014 with her husband Jude, where they bike, swim, and kayak with the dolphins.

They recently celebrated their 25th Anniversary with an adventurous trip to Alaska's Denali National Forest, the Alaskan coastline and Vancouver, BC, where they were entranced with natural wonders and wonderful people.

They are the proud aunt and uncle of twenty-four amazing nieces and nephews. Karen believes that it is an enduring tribute to the values of both families that they have all grown into such bright, fun, curious and talented individuals as young adults. It's a joy when they visit!

CONTACT INFO:
Karen Flaherty
Living by Human Design
https://livingbyhumandesign.com
Office: 386-693-4263
Karen@LivingbyHumanDesign.com

ACKNOWLEDGMENTS

I am so grateful to everyone who's helped in making this book possible. I've been supported and loved and encouraged like I've never been before. People have shown up at every turn to help in so many ways. It's hard to believe it's all come together so fortuitously and seamlessly. I was sure it was the right next step for me because it happened that way.

I'm grateful to my friends and family, my colleagues in Corporate America and in Human Design, and teachers galore.

I'm grateful to the people at Self-Publishing School, especially Chandler Bolt, Lise Cartwright and Sean Sumner, and my editor Qat Wanders, interior designer and formatter Sharon Brownlie, and the designers they suggested. I don't know how far I'd have gotten without my trusty and loyal accountability partner, Sam Thorpe, in England, who was generous and wise throughout our tandem process.

There are really hundreds of teachers, friends and colleagues who have helped me to this point. If I named them all, some would be missed. Suffice to say, it takes a team at any point to accomplish something that can help others; and this book is a testament to that fact. I thank you all and send you much love!

SELF-PUBLISHING
SCHOOL

NOW IT'S YOUR TURN
Discover the EXACT 3-step blueprint you need to become a bestselling author in 3 months.

Self-Publishing School helped me, and now I want them to help you with this FREE WEBINAR!

Even if you're busy, bad at writing, or don't know where to start, you CAN write a bestseller and build your best life.

With tools and experience across a variety niches and professions, Self-Publishing School is the <u>only</u> resource you need to take your book to the finish line!

DON'T WAIT

Watch this FREE WEBINAR now, and say "YES" to becoming a bestseller:

http://bit.ly/2zpS3zh

Getting to Know YOU"
Bonus Page

To receive a complimentary mp3 of the audiobook, please visit:
Https://LivingbyHumanDesign.com/gtkyaudio/

*

To receive a complimentary Human Design chart, please visit:
Https://LivingbyHumanDesign.com/gtkychart/
It will help you to follow along in the book much more easily, if you
have your own Human Design chart with you as you read.

Made in USA - North Chelmsford, MA
1193458_9781732594043
11.12.2020 1652